Hans Walter Wolff

Amos
the Prophet

The Man and His Background

Translated by FOSTER R. MCCURLEY

Edited, with an Introduction, by
JOHN REUMANN

FORTRESS PRESS   Philadelphia

This book is a translation of *Amos' geistige Heimat*, Volume 18 in the series Wissenschaftliche Monographien zum Alten und Neuen Testament, edited by Günther Bornkamm and Gerhard von Rad, published by Neukirchener Verlag des Erziehungsvereins, Neukirchen-Vluyn, Germany, in 1964. It is translated here by arrangement with the publisher.

Library of Congress Catalog Card Number 72–87062

ISBN 0–8006–0012–6

3238G72   Printed in U.S.A.   1-12

Contents

221.924
W85

iii

122547

Editor's Introduction

THE PROPHET Amos has long attracted attention as a vivid spokesman for God, called by Yahweh from his work as "a herdsman and a dresser of sycamore trees" (7:14) at Tekoa, south of Bethlehem, in Judah, to deliver his message of doom to the Northern Kingdom of Israel in the decade after 760 B.C. He has attracted particular interest as the figure who opens a new period in the history of Hebrew prophets and as the first of these preachers whose spoken words came to be written down and collected in a book of their own in the Bible.

Accordingly, the background of this prophet has taken on well-deserved importance. The monograph by Hans Walter Wolff, here translated for the first time, marks an important turn in the attempts by scholars to understand the provenance of Amos, his language, thought-world, and heritage in Israel and internationally. What is more, Professor Wolff's analysis, by its links with other parts of the Old Testament, raises the possibility of broader implications regarding the "wisdom movement" in the ancient Near East than his seemingly technical and limited study of the thought and rhetoric of Amos might at first suggest.

In a famous incident at the cultic shrine of Bethel, north of Jerusalem, Amos was challenged by the priest there, Amaziah, to go back to the land of Judah with his message about the end to come upon God's people (7:10 ff.; cf. 8:2). It is when Amaziah addresses him as a "seer" (*ḥōzeh*) that Amos replies with his famous speech, "I am no prophet (*nābî'*), nor a prophet's son . . ." (7:14). But he seemingly has been called to prophesy, and once he refers to a "prophetic succession" in the past (2:11 f.)—unless these verses in chapter two are an insertion by a later hand, as some scholars think. The words of Amos at 7:14 have been interpreted to mean, "I *was* not a prophet but became one on God's call" (so the ancient Greek translation; H. H. Rowley); or taken as a question, "Am I not a prophet?" (cf. J. D. W. Watts); or in the sense, "I am not a professional prophet, a member of a prophetic guild" (J. Morgenstern) but "am none-theless a different kind of prophet" (S. Cohen). (For full references to the literature referred to by the author's name or short title in this Introduction, see the bibliography "For Further Reading" at the end of this book.) Understandably, there has been debate on whether Amos was a *nābî'* (prophet) or not, and if he was, what kind of prophet, and how he fits into the overall history of prophecy.

The origins of Hebrew prophecy continue to be discussed and, in spite of new discoveries in related civilizations, remain obscure. The movement as a whole has received various interpretations. A genera-tion or two ago it was popular to portray the prophets as the champions of biblical religion and especially morality, in contrast to the priests and the cult. On this interpretation Amos has been seen as a stalwart preacher addressing God's will to corrupt cult and corrupt society. "The prophets were Protestants!" In more recent times there has been a tendency to bring the prophets into much closer association with the cult. There were, after all, cult prophets in Old Testament times, and cultic terms and ways of speaking have been detected by some scholars in the sayings of Amos. On this reading Amos becomes a cultic figure, duly installed in an office and reflecting the thought of Jerusalem or some other religious center. Or was Amos a layman, or a "loner"? All of these views have been proposed, as well as the position that stresses his call by God as the decisive thing; some sort of Tekoan "Damascus Road" experience cannot be overlooked as a decisive personal experience, but it need not be psychologized as it has sometimes been.

The particular new development concerning Amos which Professor Wolff provides is to view him more fully than had been done before in light of the traditional, proverbial wisdom, cherished in nomad desert clans and small towns, such as Amos must have known in his sojournings around Tekoa. Wandering south and east, he no doubt met Edomites and other tribes from the east, whose wisdom he learned and shared. It was a wisdom akin to what Israelite clans had revered over the centuries, with a passion for righteousness and justice, the "right way" in life. Indeed, these desert clans no doubt preserved elements from Israel's early days which had undergone development of a different sort in the cult sanctuaries or in wisdom circles at the royal court.

Thus the answer proposed by Wolff to the question of the provenance of Amos, his "geistige Heimat" as the original title put it (literally, "spiritual or intellectual home"—it is translated "cultural background" at the author's suggestion), is the oral teachings about wisdom developed in Israelite clans out of which Amos stemmed. Here, rather than in the cult, or in some psychologizing of his "call," lies a new key to interpreting certain parts of the Book of Amos.

This emphasis may well be set in a broader framework of current reappreciation of wisdom in the Bible. True, most handbooks on wisdom do not relate that theme to the prophets (e.g., the book on wisdom literature by Wood scarcely refers to examples in the prophets), and few of the existing commentaries on Amos have as yet picked up the wisdom background that Professor Wolff argued for in this monograph as early as 1964. Indeed many of the commentaries do not yet reflect the cultic background for Amos, against which Wolff argues! What James L. Mays wrote in 1959 in a survey on recent study of the Book of Amos still holds: ". . . a great part of the significant work on the prophets in general and Amos in particular has appeared in German and goes untranslated and to some degree unappropriated" (*Interpretation* 13 [1959]: 261).

Precisely because Wolff's treatment seems to signal a significant new direction, translation of this essay and consideration of its argument seem called for. Professor Dermot Ryan, now Archbishop of Dublin, in *A New Catholic Commentary* (1969), concludes, for example, that "the simple wisdom of the family or tribe" is "one of the most important sources for the prophet's thinking and it is there we should look for an understanding of his message and not to the more sophisticated circles of the cult prophets . . ." (p. 693). Even those who feel Wolff's claims extravagant grant that "scholars are taking a longer look at the interrelationship of sage and prophet" (R. E. Murphy, *Interpretation* 23 [1969]: 291). A considerable literature has evolved on wisdom, particularly as it was treasured and used in the clans of Israel. Recent technical monographs have traced its relationships to many rhetorical forms found in the Old Testament, including the prophets. At points the wisdom background is a viable alternative to positing roots in the cult or in some festival celebrating the covenant. Wisdom's influence has been claimed not only for the prophets but also in apocalyptic (e.g., by von Rad, and in the essay by von der Osten-Sacken). For details, see Father Murphy's articles and some of the titles listed under "For Further Reading" on the wisdom movement.

The connection between Amos and wisdom is not absolutely new. Almost every commentator has observed Amos was "no country bumpkin," as Charles Kraft puts it (*Interpreter's One-Volume Commentary*, p. 465), or that he seemed to know a great deal about international affairs (if all or some of the "foreign oracles" at 1:3–2:3 are genuine), or that some specific passage like 3:3–6 resembles wisdom literature (so J. M. Ward, *Amos & Isaiah*, p. 40). Almost seventy years ago William R. Harper wrote that the influence on Amos of wisdom (Harper said "wisdom literature," whereas today we reckon more with oral traditions for this period) "can scarcely be doubted" (ICC *Amos*, p. cxxxvii). In more modern times, it has been

Johannes Lindblom and Samuel Terrien, to whom Wolff rightly gives credit, who have seen Amos in light of wisdom materials.

The brief article by Terrien in the 1962 volume, *Israel's Prophetic Heritage*, is particularly noteworthy. Terrien goes briefly into eight areas where Amos reflects "the language and speech habits of the wisemen." They include (1) consecutive numerals used in pairs ("On account of three transgressions . . . yea four . . ."), what Wolff calls the "graduated numerical sequence"; (2) a reference to "Sheol" at 9:2; (3) the didactic method of using rhetorical questions; (4) the term "secret" (*sôd*) at 3:7; (5) the phrase "what is right" (*nᵉkōḥāh*, 3:10); (6) the expression "his anger tore" at 1:11 (cf. Job 18:4); and references to (7) Isaac (7:9, 16) and to (8) Beer-sheba (5:5; 8:14). Most of these Wolff takes up in detail, rejecting some as not really providing evidence and elaborating others as the basis for an interpretation of Amos used in a commentary he has prepared.

One of the strengths of Wolff's work is that it includes technical monographs such as the one before us, full-fledged commentaries where his views on each detail can be checked out, and also sermons and more popular treatments for the nonspecialist. That, at least, is the case here, for he has produced a three-hundred-page commentary on Amos and a smaller booklet for nontechnical readers, as well as this essay. His popular treatment, *Die Stunde des Amos*, includes an introduction, some exegesis ("for non-exegetes"), sermons on parts of Amos, and a translation which marks off in italics the phrases which he believes Amos's pupils added and puts into smaller type what he takes to be later additions from the next century or two.

A similar technique was applied in treating Hosea and Joel: detailed commentary and popular exposition for the general reader. In the case of Hosea, Wolff also produced an essay entitled "Hoseas geistige Heimat" (reprinted in his collected essays). Hosea's background he sees in a long line of prophets stretching throughout Israel's history, from the exodus on (cf. Hosea 12:13; 12:9 f.; 6:5; 9:7–9). While not all agree completely with this analysis (for discussion and criticism, see the article by Rolf Rendtorff, in *Journal for Theology and the Church*, 4), Wolff has made a likely case which challenges the views that each prophet was an isolated individual, and that "writing prophets" are to be sharply separated from other prophets. His endeavor in each case has been to be sensitive to the cultural background of each prophet.

To such a task Hans Walter Wolff brings all the tools of scholarly analysis, which, through careful application, often lead him to new conclusions, plus a concern for communicating his findings about a prophet's message to church and public today. Not surprisingly, his bibliography includes both highly technical, detailed works and quite simple, general presentations, including Bible study on the Book of Jonah for the 1965 Kirchentag.

Now Professor of Old Testament at Heidelberg, he was born in 1911 at Barmen, Germany, and educated at Bethel, Göttingen, and Bonn. He served as a parish pastor from 1937 to 1949 and began teaching at the Kirchliche Hochschule in Wuppertal in 1947, where he was professor from 1951 to 1959. He then became professor at Mainz (1959) and Munich (1966), before assuming his present position in 1967. In 1972 he lectured in South America and the United States.

Professor Wolff's dissertation in 1937 dealt with the citation as a form in prophetic material, a study in the prophetical manner of preaching (printed in his *Gesammelte Studien*). A second major work, on Isaiah 53 in late Judaism and early Christianity, including Justin Martyr, was written in 1942, while on study leave from military service. For over a decade he has been at work on the minor prophets in the "Book of the Twelve" (Dodekapropheton), fruits from which engage us here. For this translation he has made helpful suggestions, particularly in seeking to develop some uniformity for English renderings of German form-critical terms. His full commentaries on Hosea, Joel, and Amos are scheduled for inclusion in the Fortress Press series, "Hermeneia." As an editor, Professor Wolff has succeeded Martin Noth in directing the German commentary series BKAT, and he has recently seen through the press a festschrift presented to Gerhard von Rad just before his death.

The translation which follows is the work of the Reverend Foster R. McCurley, Associate Professor of Old Testament and Hebrew at the Lutheran Theological Seminary, Philadelphia. He holds his Ph.D. degree from Dropsie University and has also studied at Tübingen and contributed articles to festschriften and periodicals.   JOHN REUMANN
Lutheran Theological Seminary at Philadelphia

Author's Preface

THIS STUDY is a result of preparatory work for a commentary on the Book of Amos in the series, the Neukirchen "Biblischer Kommentar." In the face of the confusing plethora of literature and hypotheses, it endeavors to ascertain, from the particularity of the prophet's manner of speech, the area of life in which he is really understandable. Thus there is a limitation on what is presented here. The commentary itself will have to test in all particulars whether the result expounded here proves to be correct or where a modified view is necessary.

These observations were expounded in an earlier version for the study group of the Biblischer Kommentar series at its spring session in Neukirchen on March 24, 1964. It was the response of the colleagues gathered there which encouraged me to make it accessible in this form for a wider circle of readers. At the same time, I was moved, not least, by the hope that I would learn further from critical replies much that would be helpful for the commentary itself.

To doctoral candidate Frank Crüsemann I am grateful for help in reading proof, and to doctoral candidate Hanns-Martin Lutz for preparation of the index.

The Necessity of the Question of Background, and the Approach Toward the Answer *

THE QUESTION of the provenance of the prophet Amos must be raised anew. The prophet himself, of course, wants to be known, in the final analysis, as one who was laid hold of by Yahweh.[1] "No doubt fresh oracles kept coming to him and inspiring him."[2] But we have recognized for some time that we dare not confuse him with ecstatics whose individual identity (*Ichfunktionen*) has been extinguished.[3] After all, the autobiographical character of his reports about visions speaks against that.[4] It is as a man fully awake that he is seized. For first, with intercession in behalf of Israel he protests against the disaster envisioned, and then, as one who is himself catechized, he must put into words the picture shown by Yahweh.[5] In his speeches he still at times distinguishes clearly between

---

1. 7:15; 3:8; 7:1–8; 8:1–2.
2. Gerhard von Rad, *Old Testament Theology*, trans. D. M. G. Stalker (New York: Harper & Row), vol. 2 (1965), p. 132. Cf. "Thus says Yahweh" in 1:3, 6, 13; 2:1, 6; 3:11, 12; 5:3, 4, 16; 7:17; "Yahweh has sworn" in 4:2; 6:8; 8:7; "utterance of Yahweh" in 2:16; 3:15; 4:3 et passim.
3. I. P. Seierstad, *Die Offenbarungserlebnisse der Propheten Amos, Jesaja und Jeremia*, 2d ed. (Oslo: Universitetsforlage, 1965).
4. 7:1 f., 4 f.; 8:1 f.; 9:1; see F. Maass, "Zur psychologischen Sonderung der Ekstase," *Wissenschaftliche Zeitschrift* (Leipzig) 3 (1953/54; Festschrift Albrecht Alt): 167–71.
5. Cf. 7:2, 5 with 7:8; 8:2.

* For List of Abbreviations see p. 97.

the message from his God and his own words.[6] We witness him, even in open disputation, using astonishingly independent and personal argumentation.[7] This manner of thinking, peculiar to him, his concepts, and his language—where are they at home?[8]

Although the only biographically productive portion of the Book of Amos shows the prophet in vigorous confrontation with the priesthood of the sanctuary at Bethel, scholars have recently been inclined to regard Amos as himself an official spokesman of the cultus. Scholars are of the opinion that they can recover his language in broad strands of the cultic traditions of the Old Testament.

That this assumption could arise is not at all astonishing, considering certain clear results of research. Basic was the observation "that there is not one point in the accusations of Amos" for which a "substantive (*sachliche*) contact with the law is not present,"[9] specifically with the Old Testament law codes, beginning with the Book of the Covenant. Beyond that, proof was provided that Amos, at least on main points, "argued on the basis of apodictic law" and "at times directed his attacks expressly at casuistic law."[10]

Research proceeded on uncertain paths when an-

6. Cf. 3:9 f. with 11; 4:1 with 2 f.; 5:1 with 3; 7:16 with 17.
7. 3:3–6, 8; 7:14 f.
8. The question is necessary even though I agree with R. Smend ("Das Nein des Amos," *EvT* 23 (1963): 419 f.) that "Amos is a loner" and that we must once again pay attention to the elements that distinguish him from his people.
9. E. Würthwein, "Amos-Studien," *ZAW* 62 (1950): 10–52, especially 40 ff.; the quotation is from p. 48.
10. R. Bach, "Gottesrecht und weltliches Recht in der Verkündigung des propheten Amos," *Festschrift für Günther Dehn* (Neukirchen: Verlag der Buchhandlung des Erziehungsvereins, 1957), pp. 23–34; quotations from pp. 28 and 33.

swers were sought to the necessary question, *Where* did Amos encounter this "law"? From the points noted above and from several further observations, the conclusion was drawn that the place in which "all" gattungen and forms in the Book of Amos "have their home" is "the cultic situation of the covenant festival."[11] Indeed, it is said, Amos clothed himself with "a far-reaching office" which included "the proclamation of salvation as well as of judgment, the message to his own people as well as to foreigners"; this office is said to be "bound to the institutions of the covenant festival proclamation."[12] Thus, one would have to think of a "regular succession in office"[13] and "perhaps an accession to office complete with public ceremonial."[14] By this reasoning, Jerusalem, "as the amphictyonic center and seat of the cultic institutions," could be accepted as cultural home for Amos.[15]

Against such deductions, questions of method and substance were immediately raised.[16] For (1) only a selection of texts in Amos was investigated closely; of all the others it is simply asserted that they would all be understandable from the same sitz im leben.[17] (2)

---

11. H. Graf Reventlow, *Das Amt des Propheten bei Amos* (FRLANT, 80; 1962), p. 111. Reventlow refers above all to E. Würthwein, "Der Ursprung der prophetischen Gerichtsrede," *ZTK* 49 (1952): 1–16, and A. Gunneweg, "Erwägungen zu Amos 7, 14," *ZTK* 57 (1960): 1–16. Cf. Reventlow, p. 13.

12. Reventlow, ibid., p. 75.

13. Ibid., pp. 21 and 24.

14. Ibid., p. 30.

15. Ibid., p. 113.

16. Cf. R. Smend, "Das Nein des Amos" (cited above, note 8), pp. 404–23, and the same author's review of Reventlow's work in *TLZ* 88 (1963): 662–64.

17. 3:9 ff.; 4:1–5; no more precise treatment is given to chaps. 5 and 6 or to 8:4 ff. and 9:7 ff.

In this random selection, passages which are disputed
on literary-critical grounds play much too important
a role in the projected understanding of Amos.[18] (3)
Other passages are dealt with insufficiently on form-
critical grounds and are treated under the unfounded
supposition that "the question about prophetic forms"
means "basically the question about the prophetic
office," and that within the framework of an institu-
tion.[19] (4) If, in the attempt to establish a relationship
between the themes in Amos and ancient Israelite
legal prescriptions, verbal dependence can in no way
be proven, then much less still can a few appeals to
the so-called rituals in Amos support the argument
for an identity in gattung with conjectural formularies of the covenant cult—especially since in this
way what is quite particularly characteristic in the
language of the prophet cannot be explained.[20] (5)

18. So 3:7 (Reventlow [cited above, note 11], pp. 26 ff.); 2:4 f. (ibid.,
pp. 59 ff., 113 f.); 9:13–15 (ibid., pp. 90 ff.).
19. Ibid., p. 10. Cf. R. Smend, "Das Nein des Amos" (cited above,
note 8), pp. 418 f. The basic thesis, formulated in general terms,
"that to a form which has been coined belongs also a corresponding
sitz im leben" (Reventlow, p. 9), one would like to see proved at
Amos 7:10–17 and above all at 3:3–8. In place of such proof, the
decisive consequences are drawn, not from form-critical inquiry, but
from the occurrence of the word *nābî'*.
20. E. Würthwein (cited above, note 9), p. 48, would, and could,
say no more than that the accusations made by Amos were "sub-
stantially" (*sachlich*) in agreement with the law which has been
handed down, and R. Bach (cited above, note 10), p. 29, showed
that Amos's charges (*Vorwürfe*) were in conformity with the "basic
characteristics of apodictic law." Reventlow, however, although he
has these results before him (p. 74), thinks that he is able to establish in the visions of Amos the "ritual of receiving a vision" ("connected to a fixed ritual"[!], p. 55), in 1:3–3:6 a "ritual of the
nations" tied "to the institutions of covenant festival proclamation"
(p. 75), in 4:6–11 a "cursing ritual" (pp. 75 ff.), and in 9:13–15 a
"blessing ritual" (pp. 90 ff.). He does all this even though he can
point out at most isolated features, but not the formal elements in
a cult formula as characteristic and basic for Amos. Cf., e.g., pp. 83 ff.

What is really the chief message of the prophet, repeated in several ways—that "the end has come for my people Israel"[21]—is least of all to be understood on the basis of an office which is supposed to have been cultically practiced in similar fashion for a long time.[22] Should not (6) the meager biographical material which is available be considered to be as basic as possible? This means, above all, the reference which occurs in the conflict with the cult official Amaziah, namely, that Yahweh had taken Amos "from following the flock."[23] This hint encourages us to consider a quite different cultural background and practical function for the prophet, as an alternative to that cult-historical (*kultgeschichtlich*) interpretation of Amos's speeches, which methodologically and substantively seems to be quite debatable, at least in the extent to which it has been proposed.

We shall first of all investigate several rhetorical forms which are typical for Amos and which can scarcely be explained from the cultus (Part One). Then we shall examine the specific themes and the linguistic usage of the prophet (Parts Two and Three).

21. 8:2.

22. The appropriately directed and concrete threat of an earthquake (2:13; 8:8; 9:1), of a final panic-filled flight without deliverance (2:14 ff.; 9:1 ff.; 5:18 ff.), of an inescapable expulsion from the land (4:3; 5:27; 6:7), of inevitable, widespread death (5:1 ff., 16 f.; 6:9 f.); and Amos's simultaneous contesting against the "certitudes" of salvation history which were nurtured in the cult (3:2; 5:14, 18 ff., 21 ff.; 9:7)—these are so without comparison that it is utterly incomprehensible how a claim can be made about a man with this message that he is "continuator of a custom which existed long before him" (Reventlow [cited above, note 11], p. 116). On 5:6, 14 f. cf. R. Smend (cited above, note 8), pp. 415 f.

23. 7:15. The distinction between *ḥozeh* (7:12; 1:1) and *nābî'* (7:14) must also still be considered; cf. provisionally R. Smend (cited above, note 8), pp. 417 f. See below, p. 87.

PART ONE:

Rhetorical Forms
Characteristic of Amos

1. THE DIDACTIC QUESTION

We shall begin with the passage at 3:3–6, 8 which for some time has been defined in a basically correct way by form-critical investigation.

3 ³ Do two walk together,
    unless they have made an appointment?
  ⁴ Does the lion roar in the forest,
    when he has no prey?
  Does the lion cry out from his hiding place,[24]
    if he has captured nothing?
  ⁵ Does a bird fall to[25] the earth,
    when no missile has hit it?
  Does a snare spring up from the ground,
    when it has taken no captive?
  ⁶ Or does a man blow a horn in the city,
    and the people do not shudder?

24. The phrase "from his hiding place" might be an addition. All remaining cola in vv. 3–6 have only three beats in the first line as preserved. On the other hand, they all do include reference to a place.

25. "Snare" (RSV) is certainly an addition here, probably inserted from v. 5*b* by a transcriptional error. The Greek does not have it. In v. 5*a* the "missile" is a hunting instrument.

Or does misfortune befall the city,
and Yahweh has not done it?[26]
[8] When the lion roars,
who then is not afraid?
When the Lord Yahweh speaks,
who then does not proclaim?

It is debatable whether v. 3 is supplemental to v. 2[27] or belonged originally with what follows. It is also uncertain whether v. 8 forms a rhetorical unity with the preceding chain of questions or whether an independent section is concluded with v. 6.[28] A pro-

26. V. 7 is best understood as an interpretation which presupposes v. 6*b* as well as v. 8*b*. Its prosaic style clearly distinguishes it from the poetic context. As a theological dictum it is reminiscent, in language and outlook, of Jeremiah 23:18, 22 and, above all, of the work of the Deuteronomic historian (cf. 2 Kings 17:13, 23; 21:10; 24:2). Cf. also S. Lehming, "Erwägungen zu Amos," *ZTK* 55 (1958): 152, and W. Schmidt in his trial lecture for *Habilitation* at Mainz on February 15, 1964, which appeared in *ZAW* 77 (1965): 168–93, under the title "Die deuteronomistische Redaktion des Amosbuches." Because of the highly probable secondary character of 3:7, it seems to me not permissible methodologically to evaluate the word *sôd* as a "wisdom term" for Amos, as Samuel Terrien does ("Amos and Wisdom," *Israel's Prophetic Heritage: Essays in Honor of James Muilenberg*, ed. Bernhard Anderson and Walter Harrelson [New York: Harper & Row, 1962], p. 112).

27. Following the precedent of K. Marti, H. Gese has argued this recently, in "Kleine Beiträge zum Verständnis des Amosbuches," *VT* 12 (1962): 425, since the colon of v. 3, in distinction to the bicola of all the following verses, lacks a parallel and its imagery does not include anything of threatening character. But are not these considerations, which lead to combining v. 3 with v. 2, far more strained than if one sees disclosed by the imagery of the two travelers who have fixed an appointment in v. 3, that structure which at the end will set forth the connection of the prophet to Yahweh (v. 8*b*)? Indeed, v. 8*a* is also reminiscent of the preceding imagery of the lion in v. 4*a*.

28. So H. Gressmann, *Die älteste Geschichtsschreibung und Prophetie Israels*, SAT II, 1 ²1921, pp. 339 f., and more recently R. Smend (cited above, note 8), p. 412, note 42. Supporting this position is not only the change of meter and the interrogative style, but also the fact that already in v. 6*b* the concern is with Yahweh. But is there really achieved here any more than a didactic preparation for the conclusion? The stylistic break in the transition from v. 6 to v. 8

visional conclusion can be said to have been reached at verse 6b—as the insertion of verse 7, a doctrinal proposition, no doubt already indicates—a conclusion at 6b which finds its precise clarification in verse 8 (stressed with the help of a shortened rhythm): the disaster brought by Yahweh upon the city, which strikes terror into the people, is the message forced upon the prophet in an irresistible way.

Our concern here is quite separate from these problems of the extent and unity of the section. The idea that every misfortune in the city comes from Yahweh is not declared as a word received from God by prophetic authority. Much less is it taught on the basis of a knowledge of God which is transmitted in the cult. That Amos speaks under an overpowering compulsion from the Lord Yahweh is explained neither in terms of a cultically regulated transfer of office nor by reference to a predecessor in office. Rather in this whole disputation which he presents about the necessity of his preaching, he avails himself exclusively of a didactic form characteristic of wisdom discourse.[29] Three features are worth noting.

First is the *realm* from which the leading questions

may be intentional, in order to mark the actual conclusion with special clarity. Hence, following the direct interrogatives of the preparatory series, the conclusion is formulated in a more thetic manner by using and modifying the images from the beginning of the series. Cf. H. Gese (cited above, note 27), pp. 426 f.

29. Even Reventlow (cited above, note 11), p. 27, sees here a "series of popular wisdom sayings" (*volkstümliche Weisheitsspruchreihe*). He reproaches Weiser for failing "to draw out the form-critical consequences from his observation," but he himself does not ask how the rhetorical form in question is related to the cultic office which he has postulated. Instead Reventlow argues his point on the basis of 3:7, without being able to refute the reasons against deriving the saying from Amos; cf. note 26 above.

are taken. The compelling analogies are derived neither from a special revealed knowledge nor from a standardized history, but from the range of experience of the man "following the flock": the struggle of the animals with one another which he observes and which looms before his eyes with particular clarity in the case of the lion as the most dangerous enemy of the flock (vv. 4, 8*a*); the life of the hunter, in which he participates (v. 5); the danger of war and other misfortunes in the city on account of which the alarm horn summons him behind the walls of the fortified city (v. 6*a*); even the two travelers who have fixed an appointment for their walk (v. 3) belong in the world of the lonely path through the steppes where people scarcely meet by accident. In this realm of natural observation the experience is gleaned that every event is indissolubly bound up with another in a cause-effect relationship. It is very astonishing that along with such analogies there is raised as part of the dispute form an understanding of Yahweh as the one who originates ill fortune as well as prophetic proclamation. This is, at any rate, completely non-cultic and not at all related to salvation history. But it is typical of wisdom.[30]

With that observation attention is already focused on the second feature which has to do with the *series of comparisons* (*Reihenbildung der Vergleiche*). It is through the chain of observations that the conclusion first becomes evident. The wisdom motif is thus at

---

30. Proverbial wisdom too perceives of Yahweh as the originator even of unfortunate, evil phonomena; cf. Prov. 16:4; 22:2; 29:13; also 15:11.

work, with its preference for bringing together comparable phenomena, thus disclosing the orderings of world happenings. It is within the framework of this ordering that Amos understands his "office" of proclamation.

Third, the *interrogative form* must be regarded as a style of wisdom rhetoric. This form has instructional functions in the didactic style of wisdom discourse since it simultaneously provokes insight into, and concurrence with, the knowledge which is perceived by the series of observations.

Elsewhere, too, Amos uses this style of assenting to penetrating questions—if not in longer series, at least in double questions. The form h^a-'im, which is found in the transition of 3:3–5 to 3:6, appears again in 6:2 and 12.

Pass over to Calneh, and see!
　From there go to Hamath Rabba!
　Go down to Gath of the Philistines!
Are (h^a) you better than these kingdoms?
　Or ('im) is "your" territory greater than "theirs"?[31] (6:2)

Training in wisdom achieves self-knowledge by means of comparison. Knowledge of foreign lands belongs from of old to its specialties.[32] Wisdom raises its voice "where the paths cross" (Prov. 8:2).

31. See *BH*.

32. Cf. the satirical letter by the Egyptian official Hori from the Nineteenth Dynasty, who in the jargon of the classroom polemicizes against a colleague and questions him expressly about his geographical knowledge (Papyrus Anastasi I): "Pray, instruct me about Beirut, about Sidon and Sarepta. Where is the stream of the Litani? What is Uzu like? . . . Come, set (me) on the way southward to the region of Acre. Where does the Achshaph road come?

The form of the double question can be modified into satire:

Do horses run upon rocks?
  Or "does one plow the sea with oxen"?[33]
But you have turned justice into poison
  and the fruit of righteousness into wormwood. (6:12)

In 5:25 f., too, there occurs what is probably[34] a double question which appears in the second part to move from instructional didactic to satire:

Did you bring to me sacrifices and offerings
  the forty years in the wilderness, O house of Israel?
And (thereby) have you taken up with Sakkuth . . .
  and Kewan?
Images . . . which you have made for yourselves?

Where is such an interrogative style at home, a style which seeks to produce serious didactic insight through a series of images, but which can also easily move on into the ironic? In cultic texts we search in vain for this rhetorical form. Perhaps one could compare Psalm 50:13 to the question which is cast in the style of divine address at 5:25,

. . . Where does the mountain of Shechem come? . . . Guide *us* (*to*) know them! . . . let me know Rehob, explain Beth-Shan and Tirqa-El. The stream of Jordon, how is it crossed?" (trans. John A. Wilson in *ANET*, pp. 475–79, quotation from p. 477). Cf. Jer. 2:10 f.

33. See *BH*.

34. Cf. E. Würthwein, "Kultpolemik oder Kultbescheid?" in *Tradition und Situation* (Festschrift A. Weiser; ed. Ernst Würthwein and Otto Kaiser; Göttingen: Vandenhoeck & Ruprecht, 1963), p. 117. See this work for restoration of the text and for bibliography; on the text itself, see also *BH*.

> Do I eat the flesh of bulls?
> Do I drink the blood of goats? (Ps. 50:13)

We have yet to explain how such questions had come into cultic divine address. Here there is indeed a structural parallel to Amos 5:25 f., insofar as in the entire section (from 5:21 on) the prophet speaks the language of the "prophetic cult decree" (*Kultbescheid*).[35] That is a point to be considered. Otherwise in cultic rhetoric we know only the "pilgrim question" in the liturgies for admission to the sanctuary.[36]

> O Yahweh, who can sojourn in thy tent?
> Who can dwell on thy holy mountain?[37] (Ps. 15:1)

Or, in prophetic modification:

> With what shall I come before Yahweh
> and bow myself before God on high?
> Shall I come before him with burnt offerings,
> with calves one year old?
> Is Yahweh pleased with thousands of rams,
> with ten thousand rivers of oil?
> Shall I give my first-born for my transgression,
> the fruit of my body for the sin of my life? (Mic. 6:6 f.)

This form of "pilgrim question" allows no comparison with the chain of questions in Amos which press

35. E. Würthwein (see previous note), p. 128.
36. Cf. K. Koch, "Tempeleinlassliturgien und Dekaloge" in *Studien zur Theologie der alttestamentlichen Überlieferungen* (Festschrift G. von Rad; ed. Rolf Rendtorff and Klaus Koch; Neukirchen: Neukirchener Verlag, 1961), pp. 45–60.
37. Cf. also Ps. 24:3 and Isa. 33:14.

on to conclusions, chains which—with the exception of 5:25 f.—were taken from the completely non-cultic realms of the animal and plant worlds (Amos 3:4 f.; 6:12), of folklore (6:2), and of human relationships (3:3; 6:12*b*).

With reference to the form, direction, and content of the chains of questions in Amos, we find parallels only in genuine wisdom texts. The home of the chain of questions in Amos 3:3 ff. is readily recognizable in connection with Job 8:11 which is part of Bildad's first speech. Job 8:8 begins:

> Inquire, indeed, of bygone ages,
>   and consider the findings of the fathers!

Then in verse 11 come the questions:

> Does papyrus grow where there is no marsh?
>   Do reeds flourish without water?

Verse 13 offers the conclusion:

> Such are the paths of all who forget God.
>   The hope of the godless man shall perish.

There is still visible here the schoollike framework of such didactic questions which continued for generations in clan instruction. The variation at Amos 6:12 which passes over into bitter irony has a seemingly exact parallel at Job 6:5 f. After the first speech by Eliphaz, Job makes clear with two synonymous double questions (which are formed by *ha-'im* as in Amos) that he has brought forth his complaint not without good reason:

> Does the wild ass bray over fresh grass?
> Or does the ox low over his fodder?
> Is that which is tasteless eaten without salt?
> Is there any taste in the white of an egg?[38]

Related in content also are the questions in the words of Agur at Proverbs 30:4. From here it is not very far to the torrents of questions in Job 38–39, which, in turn, are to be seen in connection with the Egyptian polemical writing of Hori and thus call to mind the "instructional method of the classroom" (*Lehrbetrieb der Beamtenschulen*);[39] attention has already been drawn to the interest in geography and folklore at Amos 6:2.

Of course, the elevated literary style of the Egyptian schools of wisdom and the Book of Job is somewhat removed from the cultural background of Amos. But it is in this literature, nonetheless, that we encounter most precisely those didactic forms found in Amos. Is it not logical to assume that this literature preserved and further developed what can be presumed for Amos in the characteristic oral tradition of clan instructional wisdom, with its basically simpler forms?[40] Precisely there, from very early days,

38. On the uncertain meaning of the word, cf. F. Horst, *Hiob* (BKAT, 16; 1960), p. 103, and G. Fohrer, *Das Buch Hiob* (KAT, 16; 1963), p. 160.

39. See note 32 above, and cf. G. von Rad, "Job XXXVIII and Ancient Egyptian Wisdom," in *The Problem of the Hexateuch and Other Essays*, trans. E. W. Trueman Dickens (New York: McGraw-Hill, 1966), pp. 287 ff. (quote from p. 290).

40. Following suggestions by J. Lindblom, "Wisdom in the Old Testament Prophets," in *Wisdom in Israel and the Ancient Near East*, *VT* Supplement III (1955), pp. 201 ff., S. Terrien was the first to pursue the question more closely; see "Amos and Wisdom" (cited above, note 26), pp. 108–15.

natural phenomena were compared with human behavior.

The north wind produces rain,
  and a disagreeable countenance, a furtive tongue.[41]
                                        (Prov. 25:23)

When the wood is gone, the fire goes out.
  When there is no slanderer, strife ceases. (Prov. 26:20)

Also compared is the working of injustice with the bitterness of wormwood (Prov. 5:4), as in Amos 6:12 and 5:7. As a form, the expanded comparison (*Vergleichsrede*) belongs here, as Amos employs it in his saying about the Day of Yahweh:

As a man flees from a lion,
  and then a bear meets him;
he enters the house and leans against the wall,
  and then a serpent bites him.
Is not the Day of Yahweh darkness and without light?
  Gloom and without brightness? (5:19 f.)

Is it an accident that Amos illustrates his discussion of the Day of Yahweh (which was otherwise expressed in terms of great martial events)[42] with the imagery familiar to a wandering shepherd? Is it by chance that the comparison, where it attempts to portray the end which is inevitable, flows into wording which

41. This example seems to presume Egyptian backgrounds; see B. Gemser, *Sprüche Salomos*, HAT, I, 16 (²1963), p. 92.
42. Cf. von Rad, *Old Testament Theology*, vol. 2 (cited above, note 2), pp. 133–38. Also cf. H. W. Wolff, *Joel* (BKAT, 14/2; 1963), pp. 12 ff., 38 f.

concludes, for example, like the wisdom saying about the drunkard whom wine "bites like a serpent" (Prov. 23:32)? And can the transition at the conclusion, from the comparison to the question which expects insight, be found anywhere else than in the didactic of wisdom? Likewise the comparisons with the cart at harvest which tears up the earth,[43] the loss sustained by the shepherd,[44] the ever-flowing brook, and the shaking sieve[45]—all these belong basically to the same type of rhetoric and to the same conceptual world.[46] Granted, such isolated observations do not in themselves prove very much. But they round off the picture which emerged with the origin of the didactic chain of questions. The preceding observations, which have often been made individually before, have not led to clearer understandings of Amos's cultural background. This situation is probably related to the fact that some of the other specific features of Amos's rhetorical forms, which point in the same direction but perhaps permit an even more exact designation of the point of origin, have been overlooked until now.

43. 2:13. See H. Gese, "Kleine Beiträge" (cited above, note 27), pp. 417–24.

44. 3:12.

45. 5:24; 9:9.

46. It is true that the comparison saying has been handed down to us chiefly in one of the more recent collections of proverbs (Prov. 25–27), but it belongs to a type which is surely of ancient origin; on the problem cf. G. Wallis, "Zu den Spruchsammlungen Prov. 10, 1–22, 16 und 25–29," *TLZ* 85 (1960): 147 f. On the question of the antiquity of the collections, see U. Skladny, *Die ältesten Spruchsammlungen in Israel* (Göttingen: Vandenhoeck & Ruprecht, 1962), pp. 76–82 (on which, cf. O. Plöger, *Gnomon* 36 [1964]: pp. 297–300).

2. THE "WOE-CRY" (*Wehe-Ruf*)

In this regard the question about the provenance of the form of the "woe-cry" appears to me especially important. In Amos the form emerges in literature for the first time. After him it appears in the prophetic writings especially frequently in Isaiah and Habakkuk.

To begin with, the transmitted text of the Book of Amos offers the form twice:

Woe to those who desire the Day of the Lord!
Why would you have the Day of the Lord? (5:18)

Woe to those who are unconcerned about Zion,
and to those who trust in the mountain of Samaria,
the nobles of the choicest people,
who (live) "like gods in the house of Israel."[47] (6:1)

In all probability 6:3–6, with its participial constructions, is to be viewed under the "woe" of verse 1, even though verse 3b—following the insertion of verse 2—changes over to the address form:

³ (Woe to those) who put far away the evil day,
but bring forth the "year"[48] of violence,
⁴ who lie upon beds of ivory,
and stretch themselves upon their couches,
who eat the lambs from the flock
and the calves from the midst of the stall,
⁵ who bawl to the sound of the lyre
. . .[49] and invent musical instruments,

47. On the text see Reinhard Fey, *Amos und Jesaja: Abhängigkeit und Eigenständigkeit des Jesaja* (WMANT, 12; 1963), p. 11.
48. With *BH*.
49. The phrase "like David" (RSV) does not appear in the Greek.

⁶ who drink wine from jugs⁵⁰
    and anoint themselves with the choicest oil. . . .

All together there are seven participial clauses here;
the second line of the bicolon can occasionally change
into a perfect (v. 3*b*, 5*b*) or imperfect (6*aβ*) finite verb.

Precisely the same structure is found at 5:7; 6:13;
and 2:7. In each case the structure can be explained
from the form of the "woe-cry." In 5:7 a "woe" (*hôy*)
at the beginning is frequently considered as original:⁵¹

"Woe to those" who turn justice into wormwood,
    and cast down righteousness to the earth!

Many scholars accept this also at 6:13:

"Woe to those" who rejoice in Lo-debar,
    who say, "Have we not by our own strength taken
        Karnaim?⁵²

In 2:7 the possibility is not absolutely to be excluded:

(Woe to those)
who . . . "trample down"⁵³ the head of the helpless
    and bend the justice of the afflicted!⁵⁴

50. Literally, "wine skins"; elsewhere the word designates the
"basin" used in the cult (Exod. 27:3 and often); Amos is thinking
of vessels which are much larger than the usual goblet; cf. K. Galling, *Biblisches Reallexikon* (Tübingen: Mohr, 1937), cols. 316 ff.;
A. G. Barrois, *Manuel d'archéologie biblique*, I (Paris: Éditions
Auguste Picard, 1939), p. 388.

51. See *BH*. A. Weiser, *Das Buch der zwölf Kleinen Propheten, I*
(ATD, 24; ⁴1963), p. 163. V. Maag, *Text, Wortschatz und Begriffs-
welt des Buches Amos* (Leiden: Brill, 1951), in loc.

52. So Maag (cited above, note 51). Weiser attaches 6:13 to 6:1.

53. For the text, see *BH*.

54. On the character of this proverb as a "woe-cry," see Reventlow
(cited above, note 11), p. 58; also **R.** Fey (cited above, note 47),
pp. 62 f. who refers to Isaiah 10:1 f.

Granted that in these three cases the insertion of the "woe" must remain uncertain, nonetheless, that these participial clauses also belonged originally to the "woe-cry" is highly probable according to the analogy of 6:1, 3–6, as well as of 5:18.

As characteristic features of such "woe-cries," no fewer than five elements appear already in Amos:

(1) The cry begins with the "woe"; the "woe" is never repeated in the following parallel members.

(2) To the "woe" is always directly attached a plural participle, upon which, as a rule, parallel terms follow, likewise in participial form or also in finite verb forms.

(3) The person threatened with the "woe" is never addressed;[55] he is never designated by name but always and only by his deeds.

(4) It appears obvious, at least on the basis of 6:1, 3–6, that there is a series or sequence of woes.

(5) The "woe-cry" as such is not basically bound up with a specific announcement of punishment; coming disaster is itself already implied in the "woe." In Amos this assumption arises from the observation that the prophetic explication of the "woe" is attached in rather varied ways to the otherwise set form; cf. 5:18*b* with 6:7 (5:11; 6:14).

How does Amos arrive at this form of "woe-cry"? Some have attempted to deduce it in a general way from curse sentences (*Fluchsprüche*).[56] But a parallel

55. On the secondary character of the forms in 6:3*b*, see above (p. 17).
56. So C. Westermann, *Basic Forms of Prophetic Speech*, trans. Hugh Clayton White (Philadelphia: Westminster, 1967), pp. 194 ff.

worthy of consideration to the formal characteristics noted above for Amos can be found only in the dodecalogue of curses in Deuteronomy 27:15–26. Here there are present all the formal characteristics mentioned for the "woe-cry," except only that the opening word "woe" is replaced by the term "cursed." However, one cannot say that curse sentences are really encountered in this form. The "shortest and most original" form of the curse as a powerful, effective word (*Wirkwort*) is rather the statement "Cursed are you!" which parallels "Blessed are you!"[57] or the word "cursed" together with a name.[58] As powerful magical-religious oracles (*Machtsprüche*), curses as well as blessings make their way chiefly into cultic speech and become the special prerogative of the priests.[59] However, the series of curses and blessings in Deuteronomy 28, in the ancient oriental legal codes, and in the vassal treaties[60] are not, because of their conditional structure, able to explain the peculiar form of the ancient Israelite dodecalogue of curses at Deuteronomy 27:15 ff. Should these verses in Deuteronomy 27 not better be understood as a

57. So F. Horst, *Gottes Recht: Gesammelte Studien zum Recht im Alten Testament. Aus Anlass von der Vollendung seines 65. Lebensjahr*, ed. H. W. Wolff (ThB, 12; 1961), pp. 192 ff.; e.g., Gen. 3:14; 4:11.

58. Gen. 9:25; Judg. 5:23; cf. Gen. 49:7.

59. Cf. F. Horst, "Segen und Fluch" in *RGG*3 V, cols. 1649 f.

60. Cf. the epilogue of the Code of Hammurabi (*ANET*, pp. 177 ff.) or of the treaty of Murshili II with Duppi-Teshub as an example of a Hittite treaty (*ANET*, pp. 203–205; in K. Baltzer, *The Covenant Formulary*, trans. David E. Green [Philadelphia: Fortress Press, 1971], pp. 182 ff.); see M. Noth, *The Laws in the Pentateuch and Other Essays*, trans. D. R. Ap-Thomas (Edinburgh: Oliver & Boyd, 1966), pp. 118 ff. On the problem see also H. Graf Reventlow, "Kultisches Recht im Alten Testament," *ZTK* 60 (1963): 267–304.

form analogous to the "woe-cry," rather than vice versa?

An affirmative answer to this question assumes that a special prehistory of the prophetic form of the "woe-cry" can be conclusively demonstrated.

The word "woe" unquestionably has its own sitz im leben which is clearly to be distinguished from the "curse" rooted in the magical-religious realm. If a "curse" always strikes living persons, a "woe" (*hôy*) apparently applied originally to the deceased. The unnamed prophet in 1 Kings 13:30 laments over the man of God lying in the grave, "Woe, my brother!" As a general, customary cry of lamentation for the dead, such a *hôy 'āḥî* ("Woe, my brother") is attested by Jeremiah (22:18); according to Jeremiah's threat (*Drohwort*) against Jehoiakim, the lamentation for the dead carried out with such words shall be denied this king, while according to Jeremiah 34:5 a *hôy 'ādôn* ("Woe, lord") shall honor King Zedekiah after his death.

For our question about the cultural background of the "woe-cry," it is of no little importance that such a "Woe!" is employed by Amos himself as catchword of a lament for the dead.

Thus says Yahweh, the God of the armies:[61]
In all the squares the lamentation for the dead will be
       sounded,
  in all the streets they will say: Woe! Woe!
They will call the farm boy[62] to the mourning rite,
  "to the lamentation"[63] him who is expert at the woe-cry.

61. "The Lord," *adonai*, is not attested in the Greek.
62. According to H. Gese (cited above, note 27), pp. 432 f.
63. See *BH*.

In all the vineyards the lament will prevail,
  for I will stride through your midst, says Yahweh.

                                            (5:16 f.)

Here it is clear that the key term originates in mourning for the dead which occurs in families and clans. As 1 Kings 13:30 and Jeremiah 22:18 and 34:5 have shown us, this "woe-cry" of lamentation for the dead was in its simplest and original form bound up with a direct address, as was the case also with the curse. Here, too, construction of a series is not self-evident. But it perhaps becomes somewhat more understandable from the fact that the "woe" is often repeated when the lament for the dead is used. This is already hinted at by the doubling at Amos 5:16.

If the series of prophetic "woe-cries" with their plural participles should be regarded form-critically as a secondary formation of the type attested in the dodecalogue of curses at Deuteronomy 27:15 ff., then it would have to be concluded that the prophets placed the living under the "woe"—that the living who were cursed according to the terminology of the clan lament were actually considered to be already dead. The prophets would have radicalized these forms by transferring the cultic form of legal proclamation into the language of profane lamentation.

However, this view of form-critical derivation is improbable, not least because of the rarity of cultic curses in a series formed with participial clauses in the apodictic style. It can rather be shown, much more convincingly, how the series of woes were formed in the wisdom language of the clan for family instruction,[64] with the help of the main theme of the lament for the dead.

It was not the later wisdom literature which was first in formulating the question, "What is good for man while he lives?"[65] On the contrary, the oldest collections of proverbs in Israel already show that their purpose was to guide men to the right decision between the way of life and the snares of death.

> The teaching of the wise is a fountain of life,
>   to avoid the snares of death.[66] (Prov. 13:14)

> The man of understanding goes upward on life's path,
>   so that he may avoid Sheol beneath. (Prov. 15:24)

Given this inclination, it is by no means astonishing but even highly probable, that in instructional clan wisdom, deeds were placed together with harmful consequences under the "woe" in quite early times. That such series are not preserved for us in the wisdom tradition can be explained by the fact that they belonged to the typical, oral-tradition material. Like many other forms, these series have come down to us only through literary representations of the prophetic versions of these forms. In court wisdom, which served to educate princes and officials, this form seems to have receded into the background. This is true, at any rate, in the transmitted collections, which in

---

64. On what follows, cf. the fundamental study by E. Gerstenberger, "The Woe-Oracles of the Prophets," *JBL* 81 (1962): 249–63.

65. Eccles. 6:12. See W. Zimmerli, "Zur Struktur der alttestamentlichen Weisheit," *ZAW* 51 (1933): 178.

66. Similarly 14:27, where "the fear of Yahweh" replaces "the teaching of the wise."

other respects too took over much of the proverbial material of clan wisdom.

The supposition that the form of the "woe-cry" belonged originally to the instructional realm of clan wisdom is supported by at least five observations involving biblical texts.

(1) In Proverbs 23:29 f. the form is presupposed in the riddle,

> ^{29} Who has woe (*hôy*)? Who has sorrow (*'ªbôy*)?
>   Who has strife? Who has complaining?
>   Who has wounds without cause?
>   Who has redness of eyes?
> ^{30} Those who tarry over wine,
>   who come to taste mixed wine.

Note here the plural participles: *lamᵉ'aḥªrîm* ("those who tarry"), *labbā'îm* ("who come"). Together with the leading question, "Who has woe?", they presume, as familiar, "woe-cries" of exactly the same structure that we saw in Amos.[67] The continuation of the form, which has been modified for the riddle, in the developed poetry in Proverbs 23:29–35 shows that here also the old prevailing goal of instruction is reflected: "to avoid the snares of death," when it is said specifically to those for whom wine goes down all too smoothly that

> in the end it bites like a serpent (v. 32).

It is hardly an accident that Amos's "woe-cry" at 5:18 also moves into a comparison at verse 19. It de-

67. See above, pp. 17 ff.

scribes, with exactly the same words, the inevitable end when it says of the man who fled from the lion and was met by a bear, who fled with greatest diffi- culty into a house and there, in a state of exhaustion, supported himself against the wall, "a serpent bit him there." Naturally, dependence of the one proverb upon the other is not to be supposed. But the same cultural background is hardly to be contested.

(2) The existence of the "woe-cry" in wisdom is verified indirectly through the "blessing-cry" (*Heil- Ruf*). Just as cultic language knows of a series of blessings (*bārûk*) alongside a series of curses (*'ārûr*),[68] so clan pedagogy formed sayings which begin with "blessed" (*'ašrê*) alongside sayings which begin with "woe" (*hôy*). We have access to these blessings, which belong to the typical, oral material used for educa- tion, only, as in other cases, through the fact that they were taken up in later literary forms. As exact paral- lels to the "woe-cries," they appear in Psalm 106:3.

> Blessed are those who preserve justice,
>   who[69] at all times exercise righteousness.

As is usual with a "woe" (*hôy*), so here, the term "blessed" (*'ašrê*) is followed in parallel constructions in each case by a plural participle. The cry "blessed" stands, like the "woe," at the beginning of the prov- erb. The man who, finding himself on life's way, is declared blessed, is not addressed. An exposition of

68. Deut. 28; cf. Jer. 17:5 ff.
69. Plural, according to the ancient versions; see *BH*.

the promised blessing is lacking, just as the exposition of the threatened disaster is lacking in the "woe-cry." The tendency toward formation of a series is likewise to be observed. It appears that the structure corresponds in all five of the points mentioned to that of the "woe-cries" in Amos.[70] In addition, worth noting is the identity of theme at Psalm 106:3 with Amos 5:7 with respect to the parallelism of justice ($mišpāṭ$) and righteousness ($ṣᵉdāqāh$). Just as for those who foster justice and righteousness there is "blessing," so for those who reject them, there is "woe."

If the chief characteristics of such pedagogical series appear here, then Psalm 41:2 (English 41:1) offers a specific example of them.

> Blessed is he who considers the weak "and the poor,"
> on the day of judgment Yahweh will save him.[71]

To be sure, there is a clear modification here of the didactic sentence insofar as the participle is in the singular and the second line of the verse develops the "blessing." On the other hand, however, precisely this "blessing-cry" is clearly reminiscent of the parallel themes in the "woe-cries" in Amos, for whom too the man who is "weak" (*dal*), like the "poor" man (*'ebyôn*), plays a prominent role;[72] and in the "woe-cry" at 6:1 ff. the "evil day" appears in verse 3a, as here, as the day of disaster. Much as one must be warned against overestimating such isolated observa-

---

70. See above, p. 19.

71. For the text, see H. J. Kraus, *Psalmen* (BKAT, 15; 3d ed. 1966), in loc.

72. Amos 2:6 f.; 5:11 f. (cf. 4:1; 8:4–6; and below, pp. 70 ff.).

tions, nevertheless they are important in the aggregate of related linguistic uses for the overall picture.

Formation of a sequence appears at the beginning of Psalm 119, which in verses 1 and 2 also preserves the strict form of the plural participles:

> Blessed are they whose way is blameless,
>> who walk in the instruction of Yahweh.
> Blessed are those who keep his testimonies,
>> who seek him with their whole heart.[73]

The slight changes in the participial style, as in the transition to the finite verb, we observed also in Amos 6:3, 5 and 5:7. Although in Psalm 119 the repetition of *'ašrê* ("blessed") may be influenced by the effects of straining somewhat the alphabetic acrosticon, the same does not hold for the identical repetition in Psalm 32:1 f. and 84:5, 6, 13, and in Psalm 128:1 f.:

> Blessed is everyone who fears Yahweh,
>> who walks in his ways!
> What your hands have created, surely you will eat it.
>> Blessed be you! Prosperity be yours!

The continuation of the psalm, which deals, after fruitful labor, with the blessing of children, shows especially beautifully that the home of the themes in the "blessing-cry" is in the life of the family and of the clan. Only the second half of the psalm, with its "blessing from Zion," is significantly different. This change of scene shows that rhetorical forms originally

---

73. Psalm 1 freely expands the old form in that it forsakes the participial style.

at home in clan life were taken over into the priestly language of the central cult. According to Psalm 128 the congratulatory formula (*Gratulationsformel*), cultivated in the clans, might have had its original sitz im leben in the birth of a child; this would correspond to the "woe" having its setting in the lament for the dead. But then the congratulatory formula was likewise transferred into the forms of etiquette found in the court circles schooled in wisdom. Thus the Queen of Sheba congratulates King Solomon:

> Blessed are your wives! Blessed are your servants,
>> who continually stand before you,
>> who listen to your wisdom. (1 Kings 10:8)

Already evident in the development of the congratulatory form are the plural participles, which are characteristic of the formation of a series of "blessing-cries" employed in instruction.

The occurrence of "blessing-cries" in collections of proverbs—even though scanty—may confirm conclusively their unquestionable provenance in wisdom and clarify their parallelism with the "woe-cries."

> He who gives heed to the word will prosper,
>> and he who trusts in Yahweh will be blessed.
>>> (Prov. 16:20)

Here the blessing is delayed till the end. In Proverbs 8:32–36 a sequence occurs with the repeated use of "blessed" (RSV "happy") which might originally have been even clearer if verse 32*b* and verse 34*a* were juxtaposed.[74] The expansion of this late formulation shows that it seeks to serve the discovery of the path to life (v. 35), just as the antithesis (v. 36) gives warning about the snares of death. Sharp antitheses are exhibited by a cry of blessing found in one of the older[75] collections of proverbs:

Blessed is the man who preserves reverence,
    but whoever hardens his heart falls into misfortune.
(Prov. 28:14)

Thus parallels in structure and content to the "blessing-cries" (*'ašrê*) confirm that the home of proverbs of woe is in wisdom. That the prophet Amos took up only the form of the woe-sayings (*hôy*), but not the "blessing-cries," is based, of course, on the nature of the message which was commissioned to him.

(3) In at least two examples we find further clues for the claim that instructional wisdom could place "woe-cries" and "blessing-cries" in antithetical combination. The first occurs in the Book of Ecclesiastes:

"Woe"[76] to you, O land, whose king is a child,
    whose princes gorge themselves in the morning!
Blessed are you, O land, whose king is a nobleman,
    whose princes eat at the proper time
        with good manners and not like drunkards!
(Eccles. 10:16 f.)

---

74. So B. Gemser (cited above, note 41), in loc. An *'ašrê*-series within the frame of a numerical sequence (*Zahlenspruch*) is still clearly recognizable in Sirach 25:7–11; see note 97.

75. According to U. Skladny (cited above, note 46), pp. 76–79.

76. See *BH*.

That such an antithetical arrangement was to have been found already in earlier pedagogical wisdom can be presumed from use of the form in Isaiah 3:10 f.[77]:

"Blessed"[78] is the righteous man! it goes well for him,
   for the fruit of their deeds they will eat.
Woe to the wicked! for it goes ill for him,
   the deed of his hands will be his due.

Like the antithesis of "good-evil," so also the antithesis of "righteous man–wicked man" is typical of wisdom and is especially common in the oldest collection preserved for us.[79]

Correspondence of the "blessing-cry" to the "woe-cry" is thus verified, not only indirectly but also directly. In this way further support is gained about the origin of the "woe-cry" from the language of instructional wisdom.

(4) Isaiah confirms our suppositions in a major and extensive way. In 5:8–24 and 10:1–4 there is preserved for us a series of seven short "woe-cries." These are followed in chapters 28–31 by further "woe-cries" (*hôy*) which are developed more fully and apparently stem from a later time.[80] The first series,

---

77. The saying is usually regarded as secondary, and is certainly so in its present context. In view, however, of the frequent use of the "woe-cry" form by Isaiah himself (see below), the question can be raised whether one should not expect the saying to have come at least from the prophet's close circle of disciples (Isa. 8:16).

78. See *BH*.

79. Cf. U. Skladny (cited above, note 46), pp. 7 ff., for evidence concerning the frequency of the antithetical pair *rāšā'-ṣaddîq* in Proverbs 10–15.

80. *hôy*, with participles attached in a series, occurs in Isaiah at 5:8, 11, 18, 20, 21, 22; 10:1; further, 28:1; (29:1); 30:1; 31:1; as an

to which we limit ourselves here, shows exactly the same structural characteristics which we listed in Amos. In particular it is apparent, because of the formula used to make the connection (most clearly at 5:9), that the amplifying statements about punishment do not self-evidently belong to the original form of the "woe-cries." This is clear from the fact that such notices of punishment are completely lacking in the three "woe-cries" at 5:18–21. Further, even in the particulars of the word choice, the themes are reminiscent not only of the corresponding language in Amos, but at the same time of the parallels from wisdom literature.[81] I draw attention only to the words about the drunkard (Isa. 5:11 f., 22; cf. Amos 6:5 f.; Prov. 23:30), to the typically wisdom antitheses of good-evil, bitter-sweet (Isa. 5:20; cf. Amos 5:14 f.; 8:10; Prov. 27:7), and not least to the direct allusions to the "wise" and "understanding" (Isa. 5:21).

(5) The final, and terminologically the most direct, evidence of the origin of the "woe-cries" in the wisdom tradition comes from Habakkuk 2:6–19. The five woe-sayings (*hôy*) which are joined together here

isolated expression: 1:4, 24; 10:5; 18:1. J. Fichtner, "Jesaja unter den Weisen," *TLZ* 74 (1949): 75–80, has shown convincingly Isaiah's relationship with wisdom and has even recognized features of content in the "woe-cries," but he failed to see that the form of the "woe-cry" as such belonged to wisdom. This form-critical relationship was demonstrated convincingly for the first time by Gerstenberger (cited above, note 64).

81. R. Fey (cited above, note 47) has pointed out significant parallels between Isaiah 5:11–13 and Amos 6:1–7. But he failed to come to the conclusion that Amos, too, stands within the wisdom tradition, although he did have it basically in mind for Isaiah, following the suggestions of Fichtner (cited above, note 80). See below, pp. 80 ff.

no longer, to be sure, display the pure basic form; they depart from it by using singular, instead of plural, participles. However, in view of the fact of series formation, the origin from the same realm as the woes in Amos and Isaiah is not to be denied. Add to this the related themes: heaping up of unjust wealth (2:6), pursuit after evil gain (2:9), building with blood (2:12), and again excessive drinking (2:15) are listed as deeds which bring disaster. Form-critically, the fact is decisive that in the introduction to the series, these "woe-cries" are expressly characterized as wisdom material by the use of the catchwords *māšāl* ("proverb"), *mᵉlîṣāh* ("satire"), and *ḥîdôt* ("riddle"); see Habakkuk 2:6*a*; cf. Proverbs 1:6.

Thus the origin of the "woe-cries" in the realm of wisdom may be considered established. They originated parallel to the corresponding "blessing-cries." Both forms together served to guide the younger generation to find the path of life and to avoid the snares of death. The initial position of "woe" or "blessed," with a plural participle immediately following, which names the deed leading to death or to life; formation in series; lack of direct address and of further explication of the disastrous or happy consequences—these are all characteristics of the basic form. Nothing indicates that Amos learned this form anywhere else than from the fathers of the clan, least of all from priests or other cult officials in a central covenant cultus.

Derivation of the "woe-cries" from the curse sayings must therefore be rejected.[82] Nonetheless, the dodecalogue of curses at Deuteronomy 27:15 ff. should not be seen in isolation from the development of the series of "woe-cries." Participial structure, formation of series, and theme argue rather for the assumption that here a transposition has taken place of the woe-sayings (*hôy*), from the ethos of clan wisdom of the old Israelite tribes into the cultic language of the sacral tribal confederation.[83] Amos is witness for the fact that in the clans, even in the eighth century, the will of Yahweh found forms of proclamation other than those fostered at the great sanctuaries. This is especially probable for the circles of those families who lived "following the flock" as Amos did.

For the early period of Israel an essential insight has been growing in scholarly circles:

> The cultic tribal confederation does not serve as principle of interpretation for the whole life of Israel before and with Yahweh in the premonarchic period; the most grandiose and most effective expression of this life, "the war of Yahweh," probably had nothing fundamentally to do with the amphictyony, but stemmed from

82. In this regard E. Gerstenberger, "Woe-Oracles" (cited above, note 64), p. 250, is correct, over against C. Westermann, *Basic Forms* (cited above, note 56), pp. 190 f.

83. This would be to move in a direction similar to that of K. Elliger and Erhard Gerstenberger. According to Elliger, "Das Gesetz Leviticus 18," *ZAW* 67 (1955): 1–25, the development runs from an ordering for the social life of the clan (*Grossfamilie*) to the cultic proclamation of the community of Yahweh; for Gerstenberger, *Wesen und Herkunft des "apodiktischen Rechts"* (WMANT, 20; 1965), the direction is from prohibitions of the clan ethos to the religious proclamations at the great festivals of Israel and to the great collections of commands and prohibitions in the "covenant formula" of the whole community of Yahweh.

another root and remained for a long time non-institutional in the highest degree.[84]

The corresponding point is to be borne in mind for the period of Amos. It is erroneous to wish to see almost everything—and precisely even the beginnings of classical prophecy—derived from a problematic central cult of the covenant (*Bundeskult*). Instead, the didactic forms of questions and the "woe-cries" show us a language which was concerned not with cult officials, but in a very living way with clan chiefs, elders, and fathers in the educational life of groups who dwelled and wandered about a long way off from the great sanctuaries. Thus it is no longer at all strange if, using "woe-cries," Amos discusses not only themes like maintaining justice and preserving righteousness, drinking wine, arrogance, self-confidence, and luxury, but also the theme of the "Day of Yahweh," which was at home in the tribal traditions about the war of Yahweh, and indeed, precisely in the language, and employing material with the outlook (*Anschauungsmaterial*), of clan wisdom.

3. THE NUMERICAL SEQUENCE (*Zahlenspruch*)

In Amos's oracles against the nations there appears a characteristic form: the graduated numerical sequence.[85] Within Amos's particular form of pro-

84. R. Smend (cited above, note 8), p. 421; cf. specifically R. Smend, *Yahweh War & Tribal Confederation*, trans. from the 2d ed. by Max Gray Rogers (Nashville & New York: Abingdon, 1970).
85. The numerical sequence has been discussed in detail by W. M. W. Roth, "The Numerical Sequence $x/x + 1$ in the Old Testament," *VT* 12 (1962): 300–11; and by Georg Sauer, *Die Sprüche Agurs: Untersuchungen zur Herkunft, Verbreitung und Bedeutung einer biblischen Stilform unter besonderer Berücksichtigung von Proverbia c. 30* (BWANT, 84; 1963).

claiming judgment (*Gerichtsverkündigung*) over the nations and over Israel, this element appears, just as the didactic question and the "woe-cry" do, only in pointing out guilt.

> Thus says Yahweh,
>> For three transgressions of Damascus,
>>> and for four, I will not take it back. . . . (1:3)

Similarly introduced are the oracles about the Philistines (1:6), Ammonites (1:13), Moabites (2:1), and about Israel (2:6); in secondary passages,[86] also about Tyre (1:9), Edom (1:11), and Judah (2:4).

Whence does Amos derive this curious form, which speaks of three and four offenses, only one of which, however, as a rule is pursued—a peculiarity which strengthens our impression that the introductory formula is part of a definite fixed pattern? What is the pattern introducing the several oracles against the nations, which for Amos is self-evident but for us is quite strange?

The graduated numerical sequence, which alone comes under consideration here for comparison, is characterized by the feature that it brings together phenomena generally comparable. Outside of the Old Testament, the device has been traced thus far in only two places: in Ugarit and in the *Words of Ahiqar*.[87] In every case it appears with the introduc-

---

86. The differences between the sequences at 1:9–12 and 2:4 f. are too great, in terms of form and content as over against context, to allow assertion of authorship by Amos; cf. A. Weiser (cited above, note 51), pp. 138 ff.; more specifically, W. Schmidt in the work cited previously (note 26).

87. Cf. G. Sauer (cited above, note 85), pp. 64–69.

tory numerical sequence, "two-three." The Ugaritic passage[88] groups together in threefold fashion examples of base conduct at a banquet; the Ahiqar passage,[89] three kinds of conduct which please Shamash, having to do with enjoyment of wine, wisdom, and secrecy. These remote texts point, therefore, even at first glance, to the realm of instructional wisdom, which we met in the rhetorical forms studied previously.

The Old Testament itself offers extensive comparative material. From the numerical sequence "one–two" in Psalm 62:12 f. (English, 11 f.),

> Once Yahweh has spoken,
> twice I have heard,
> that protection is with God,
> and with you, Lord, is favor,

to the sequence "nine–ten" in Sirach 25:7–11, almost all intermediate stages are found. The sequence "three–four," which occurs in Amos, appears especially often. In Proverbs 30 alone it occurs four times (vv. 15 f., 18 f., 21–23, and 29–31); it crops up later in Sirach 26:5 f. Unfortunately nothing reliable can be determined any longer concerning the origin of Proverbs 30, since neither the association of 30:15 ff. with "the words of Agur, son of Jakeh of Massa" (Prov.

88. Cyrus H. Gordon, *Ugaritic Textbook* (Analecta Orientalia, 38; Rome: Pontifical Biblical Institute, 1965), p. 170 (Gordon 51 iii 17–21); *ANET*, p. 132 (II AB iii 17–21).

89. *ANET*, p. 428. The passage is not included in the fragmentary translation in *The Apocrypha and Pseudepigrapha of the Old Testament*, ed. R. H. Charles (Oxford: Clarendon Press, 1913, reprinted 1963, 1965), 2:779.

30:1), nor the origin of that phrase can be explained.[90] Be that as it may, these numerical sequences do not belong to one of the great collections which were produced at the Jerusalem court (cf. 10:1; 25:1). They thus could just be associated with that "wisdom of the sons of the east" which is expressly distinguished from the great courtly "wisdom of Egypt" in 1 Kings 5:10 (English 4:30). It is this type of wisdom that is not from the court to which the "wisdom of the Edomites" also belonged; the Edomites were a people who flourished not far from the region where Amos of Tekoa lived, and their wisdom is often mentioned in the Old Testament.[91] The content of the numerical sequences in Proverbs 30 is, as a whole, more strongly reminiscent of the world of people living in a seminomadic state and of small clan units than it is of the great world of court culture.

To begin with, the numerical sequences simply place together phenomena which can be compared, without ethical concerns entering in. The world is

90. Cf. H. Ringgren, *Sprüche* (ATD 16/1; 1962), pp. 114 ff.; B. Gemser (cited above, note 41), pp. 103 ff., who along with H. Schneider, *Sprüche-Prediger-Hoheslied* (HBK, 1962), p. 158, argue against the unity of the chapter. G. Sauer (cited above, note 85), pp. 92 ff. and O. Eissfeldt, *The Old Testament: An Introduction*, trans. P. R. Ackroyd (New York: Harper & Row, 1965), pp. 475 f., deal with Proverbs 30 as a unity.

91. On the wisdom of the Edomites, cf., besides 1 Kings 5:11 (English 4:31), Jer. 49:7; Obadiah 8; and Job 2:11. Agur is to be located preferably "between Edom and Arabia, in the vicinity southeast of Judah" (H. Schneider, cited in previous note, p. 158), where the travels of Amos with his herd and as a trimmer of sycamore trees could easily have led. The slave who becomes king (30:22) and the comparison of the king simultaneously with the lion, the cock, and the he-goat (according to 30:30 f.) are more easily conceived in this area than in the great schools for princes and officials in the major cities.

regulated in such a way that one thing is related to another.[92]

> There are three things which are never satisfied;
>   four never say, "Enough":
> Sheol, the barren womb,
>   the earth which does not get enough water,
>   and the fire which never says, "Enough."
>   (Prov. 30:15b–16)[93]

Yet even in these sayings, the problems of human social life with which Amos was concerned come to the fore.

> Under three things the earth trembles,
>   . . .[94] four it cannot endure:
> Under a slave when he becomes king,
>   a fool when he is satisfied with food,
> under an unloved woman when she gets married,
>   a maid when she displaces her mistress. (Prov. 30:21–23)

As conduct toward one's fellow men which is condemned, things detested by Yahweh are grouped together in the numerical sequence at Proverbs 6:16–19:

> Six things Yahweh hates,
>   and seven are an abomination to him:
> haughty eyes, a false tongue,
>   hands which shed innocent blood,

92. Cf. von Rad, *Old Testament Theology* (cited above, note 2), vol. 1 (1962), pp. 425 f.

93. Against interpretation of Proverbs 30:15a α as a superscription, proposed by Ringgren (cited above, note 90), pp. 116 ff., cf. the explanation—correct in my view—of H. Schneider, "Die 'Töchter' des Blutegels in Spr. 30, 15" in *Lex Tua Veritas* (Festschrift H. Junker; ed. H. Gross and F. Mussner; Trier: Paulinus-Verlag, 1961), pp. 257–64; also Schneider's commentary (cited above, note 90), p. 161.

94. See *BH*.

>   a heart which devises evil plans,
>   feet which hasten to evil,
> one who breathes out lies as false witness,
>   one who sows strife among brothers.

Such abominations are obviously related to those which Amos severely criticizes in his oracles against the nations.

Before we look at still further material, let us turn to the question, How can it be explained that Amos, in spite of the announcement of "three" and "four" outrages, regularly mentions only one? Previously we determined that on occasion the higher number also was carried through. We now go back once again to Proverbs 30. The two numerical sequences which have not yet been dealt with offer a peculiarity:

> There are three things too wonderful for me,
>   four which I do not understand:
> the way of an eagle in the sky,
>   the way of a serpent on a rock,
> the way of a ship on the high seas,
>   the way of a man with a maiden. (Prov. 30:18 f.)

Here it is striking that only the fourth phenomenon has to do with human social life. The particular mystery of the association of man with woman is introduced in light of extrahuman phenomena which have in common the fact that they signify a way which is not fixed, which is not constructed as a highway, a way which is always to be attained for the first time. So wonderful, so little to be comprehended beforehand, so ever to be found anew, is the way of a man with a woman. One has the impression that the first three phenomena are introduced only to bring into the spotlight the human happening in the fourth. The same thing is probable at Proverbs 30:29–31.

> There are three things which walk with stately tread,
>   and four which walk nobly:
> the lion, the warrior among the animals,
>   who turns back before none;
> the cock as he struts, and the he-goat,
>   and the king "when he rises before his people."[95]

Here too it is essential to get to the last line concerning the human element, which is compared with the aforementioned three animals.

In view of the numerical sequences previously cited and discussed, it is improper to argue that this scheme always applies. But at least three later examples cited below point in the same direction.

> Before three things my heart is afraid,
>   and before a fourth I am very frightened:
> the slander of a city, the gathering of a mob, and false
>   accusation.
>   All these are more miserable than death.
> But sorrow of heart and woe produce a jealous wife,
>   and the scourge of her tongue forces itself on all.
>
> (Sirach 26:5–6)

Here the fourth frightening thing is clearly elevated above the first three by the breadth and exactness of the description. It is precisely the fourth which the sequence stresses as something especially distressing against the background of general troubles. The Greek text brings this out here, as elsewhere in Sir-

---

95. Read *lāqûm 'al-'ammô*; for text and translation, cf. Gemser (cited above, note 41), in loc.

ach, just as in the four numerical sequences in Proverbs 30:15 ff. and in Job 5:19, by using the cardinal number ("three") in the first instance, but the ordinal ("fourth") in the second. In that way too a stress is placed on the final member.[96] The same is true of Sirach 26:28:

> Over two things my heart is troubled,
>   and because of a third anger comes over me:
> when a well-to-do man becomes poor and must starve;
>   when famous people fall into disgrace;
> when, however, one turns from righteousness to sin,
>   him will the Lord designate for the sword.

Apparently the weight here too lies on the message in the last lines. Finally, such an emphasis on the final element in a series is found incontrovertibly in the longest example at Sirach 25:7–11:

> Nine things I praise in my heart,
>   but the tenth I speak forth with my tongue:
> Happy is he 1) who has joy in his children,
> 2)   who lives to see the downfall of his foes,
> 3)   [8] who has a clever wife.
> 4)   Happy is he who has not simultaneously hitched
>   ox and ass for plowing,
> 5)   who does not come to ruin through his tongue,
> 6)   who must not serve an inferior.
> 7)   [9] Happy is he who has gained a friend,
> 8)   who speaks to ears which listen.
> 9)   [10] How great is he who has found wisdom!
> 10)   But none is greater than he who fears the Lord.
>   [11] The fear of the Lord surpasses everything.
> Whoever holds it fast—to whom can one compare him?

---

96. On the problem, with citation of further literature, cf. G. Sauer (cited above, note 85), pp. 69 f.

After the first eight phenomena which appear quite similar in style and in content[97] and which basically cite experiences among men, the ninth, clearly elevated in style, already shows movement toward a climax. Yet it only helps shape, in quite unparalleled fashion, the climactic ascent to the tenth element, the incomparability of which is then expressed over and over.

If one surveys these total findings from the numerical sequences, the result for Amos is, first of all, that the origin of this feature of the numerical sequences in the cycle of oracles against the nations (*Völkerspruch*) can be found only in the rhetorical forms of wisdom. The comparative material shows amply that the form of the numerical sequence served—not exclusively but chiefly—to present or to illuminate social phenomena (Prov. 30:21–23; 30:18 f.; 30:29–31; Sirach 25:7 ff.); moreover, it served to set forth vice catalogues which summed up various kinds of behavior especially inimical to society (Prov. 6:16–19; Sirach 26:5–6). In a manner similar to the "woe- and blessing-cries," the numerical sequence can also, there-

---

97. In the received Greek text *makarios* ("happy") appears at the beginning of vv. 8 and 9. It probably stood at the beginning of v. 7*b*, too, but has been changed to *anthrōpos*, probably as a result of reading a mutilated *'ašrê* in the Vorlage as *'iš*. Thus there is present in our text a coupling of a numerical sequence with an *'ašrê*-series in which at present three assertions are pulled together under a "Happy!" In this way the tenth is once again powerfully lifted into prominence. For the text, cf. R. Smend, *Die Weisheit des Jesus Sirach* (Berlin: Reimer, 1906), p. 226. On the problem of the borrowing of older traditions in Sirach, cf. now W. Fuss, *Tradition und Komposition im Buche Jesus Sirach* (dissertation at Tübingen, 1963; reviewed in *TLZ* 88 [1963]: 948 f.).

fore, serve for instruction in wisdom, even if not in the same exclusive sense as those forms. Amos was undoubtedly familiar with this kind of numerical sequence from the clan ethos in which he had grown up.[98]

Amos's usage must have developed from that type in which the emphasis came only in the last member —the type we encountered in Proverbs 30:18 f., 29– 31; Sirach 25:5 f., 7–11, and 26:28. For the fact can then be explained that in the accusations in the oracles against foreign nations, only one outrage is pursued. It is precisely the fourth one which mentions the climax of the sequence, the most horrendous of abominations.[99]

Only as an appendix do we now mention that solitary late example, according to which numerical sequences could also have been concerned with foreign nations:

> Against two (pagan-)nations my soul is vexed,
> but the third is no people (of God) at all:

98. The predominance of the "three–four" numerical sequence in usage in the clan ethos is to be explained along the same lines as were recognized by E. Gerstenberger, *Wesen und Herkunft* (cited above, note 83), pp. 77–88. Gerstenberger noted that the prohibitions were formed predominantly in pairs of commands and then in series of three and four. "Almost all longer lists in some way go back to smaller units" (p. 88). The late combination of a numerical sequence and *'ašrê*-series in Sirach 25:7–11 (see previous note) can be explained by the fact that originally the series of blessings and woes served a function in the wisdom pedagogy similar to that which the numerical sequences served.

99. The tension between the number mentioned at the beginning of the numerical sequence and the actual number of distresses cited in Job 5:19–21 may be due to different reasons. Here a secondary expansion is also to be sought; cf. F. Horst, *Hiob* (cited above, note 38), pp. 87 f., and G. Fohrer, *Hiob* (cited above, note 38), p. 154.

> the inhabitants of Seir and of Philistia,
> and the infamous (pagan-)people who dwell
>   in Shechem.[100]   (Sirach 50:25 f.)

Here too the last member receives the dominant emphasis.

The fact that the discrepancy between numerical structure and its execution may be understood on the basis of the development of the numerical sequence is, in view of the absence otherwise of this inconsistency,[101] still no adequate explanation. Rather it must be seen that in Amos generally there is a violation of the form of the numerical sequence: Amos subordinates his components to the saying which threatens punishment (*Strafandrohungswort*) for the purpose of demonstrating guilt and establishing the basis for the punishment. This is no different from what he does with the "woe-cries" in 5:18–20 and 6:1–7 which become the vehicle for the announcement of judgment (*Gerichtsankündigung*).

But precisely in this way it becomes apparent that his inherited thinking and the rhetorical forms peculiar to him are at home, not in the curse- and blessing-formulas or in other rituals of the cultus of the great sanctuaries, but in the wisdom language of the clan used for instruction.

4. THE EXHORTATION SPEECH (*Mahnrede*)

On the basis of our previous observations, one must of necessity raise the question whether the par-

---

100. The proverb distinguishes precisely the *góy* in vv. 25*a* and 26*b* from the *'am* in 25*b*; cf. A. Cody, "When is Chosen People called a góy?", *VT* 14 (1964): 1–6.
101. On the single exception at Job 5:19–21, see note 99.

ticular form of exhortation speech used by Amos does
not spring from the same roots in wisdom. Very rarely
does this prophet exhort: 4:4 f.; 5:4–6, 14 f. On the
whole, exhortations are hardly to be observed in
Amos. To exhort and to warn was apparently not his
distinctive commission as prophet. But where he does,
the question of the form-critical character of such
speeches is forced upon us.

The form no doubt occurs most clearly at 5:14 f.

Seek good and not evil,
    that you may live,
and let it be so—Yahweh . . .[102] be with you—as you say.
Hate evil and love good!
    Enforce justice in the gate!
Perhaps Yahweh . . .[102] will be gracious to a remnant of
            Joseph.

Two things are characteristic for the form of this exhortation. First, the repeated antithetical form: "Seek
good and not evil!" (v. 14); "Hate evil and love
good!" (v. 15). The same parallel ordering of imperative and prohibition is present in 5:4 f.: "Seek me.
. . . Do not seek Bethel! . . ." Antithetical parallelism,
as is well known, is quite characteristic of the wisdom
mode of expression. What is probably the oldest collection of proverbs (Prov. 10–15) offers more than
ninety per cent antithetically formed proverbs, and
the collection that is probably second oldest (Prov.
28 f.) more than eighty per cent.[103] Thus, on a purely
statistical basis, nowhere in the entire realm of Old

102. Cf. *BH*.
103. Thus U. Skladny (cited above, note 46), p. 68.

Testament literature does the contrast "good-evil" and "hate-love" play such an important role as in the wisdom writings, particularly in proverbs. To be sure, in the proverbs handed down to us, the exhortation speech recedes far behind the declarative forms,[104] whereas Egyptian wisdom, "in keeping with its whole didactic aim, is almost exclusively in admonitory form (*Mahnrede*)."[105] The older brief series of prohibitions, absorbed into the great covenant formulations of the Pentateuch, and their partial supplementation through positive commands (*Gebote*),[106] can be explained by the fact that in clan instruction the exhortation speech took in a larger area than the wisdom proverb, which has come down to us in written form, allows us to realize. While the larger series which were collected for public proclamation usually had the form of synonymous parallelism, such as the dodecalogue of curses, the decalogue, and parts of the Book of the Covenant and of the Holiness Code (e.g., Lev. 18) exhibit, family instruction inclined to parallelism which was concise, antithetical, and applied generally. No doubt the relationship of many sections in Leviticus 19 with proverbial passages, shows that "the place of this tradition has been the old Is-

---

104. A noteworthy parallel to the scarcity of the exhortation speech in Amos. The matter surely has various sorts of causes, which, however, demand further consideration and perhaps are nonetheless related, insofar as, in ancient Israelite wisdom, it is the order established by Yahweh which governs the declarations; in prophecy, his future deeds.

105. G. von Rad, *Old Testament Theology*, vol. 1 (cited above, note 92), p. 430.

106. E. Gerstenberger, *Wesen und Herkunft* (cited above, note 83), pp. 43–45; cf. Lev. 19:9 f.; Deut. 25:13–15.

raelite family."[107] Certainly the assertion that only
the priests had the right to speak "apodictically" does
not at all coincide with the facts.[108] The ancient Israelite clan ethos not only made its way into the great
cult formulations, but also lived on in the family and
there maintained even more strongly its wisdom
structure, as attested to us in Amos chiefly in the
antithetical form.

The other characteristic of form in Amos 5:14 f. is
the result clause (*Folgesatz*) which, together with exhortation and warning, stamps the peculiar structure
of this type of exhortation speech.

> Seek the good . . . in order that you might live!
>   Enforce justice in the gate!
> Perhaps Yahweh will be gracious . . . !

The exhortation is expressly underlined by the fact
that insight is awakened into the result of the deed
which is expected or dreaded. "That you might live"
is the final goal of all wisdom teaching.

> Listen to advice and accept instruction,
>   that you might become wise at your end. (Prov. 19:20)

> The wise man goes upward on life's path,
>   that he might avoid Sheol below. (Prov. 15:24)

In both places the word which means "in order that"
(*lema'an*) in Amos (5:14) appears. But usually the

---

107. So Chr. Feucht, *Untersuchungen zum Heiligkeitsgesetz* (Arbeiten zur Theologie, 20; Berlin: Evangelische Verlagsanstalt, 1964),
p. 115.
108. Correctly emphasized by Feucht (cited above, note 107), pp.
108 ff.

result is attached by a simple copula, as Amos himself also employs it.

Seek me, that you may live![109] (5:4)

> (RSV, "Seek me and live")

Seek Yahweh, that you may live! (5:6)

> (RSV, ". . . and live")

Or in ironic form:

Seek Bethel, and (i.e., that you may) transgress,
  Gilgal, and (i.e., that you may) transgress even more.
                                                    (4:4)

Precisely in this style the teacher of wisdom exhorts:

Keep (sing.) my commandments and (i.e., that you [sing.]
  may) live!   (Prov. 4:4 = 7:2)

The context shows how such exhortation takes place within the chain of generations in the family.

Leave foolishness, that you may live!
  Walk in the way of insight! (Prov. 9:6)
Walk with wise men that you may become wise!
  But whoever walks with fools will suffer harm!
                                            (Prov. 13:20)

The older empirical wisdom had constantly placed together in its maxims the deed and its consequence:

Strive[110] after righteousness, for it leads to life,
  but he who pursues evil to his death. (Prov. 11:19)

---

109. After an imperative a result clause is formed with the indirect imperative; so 1 Kings 1:12; 2 Kings 5:10; on Gen. 12:1*b* cf. H. W. Wolff, "The Kerygma of the Yahwist," *Interpretation* 20 (1966): 137, n. 28, for further information.

110. Cf. Gemser (cited above, note 41), in loc.

The desire of the righteous ends in nothing but good,
  the hope of the wicked, in wrath. (Prov. 11:23)

On the path of righteousness is life,
  but the way of "apostasy"[111] leads "to" death.
                                             (Prov. 12:28)

From this world of wisdom thought and speech, the
exhortation sayings of Amos become thoroughly understandable, especially in regard to their antithetical
structure and their references to consequences, which
are described for the purpose of awakening insight.

The exhortations in Amos are clearly enough distinguished from two other types of exhortation sayings. To date, Amos 5:4–6, 14 f. has been interpreted
mostly as "imitations of priestly Torah."[112] But
priestly Torah, as exhortation speech, so far as we
can see, is not at all accompanied by reference to the
consequences. Rather, through allusion to the will of
Yahweh, it is grounded in heilsgeschichte or simply
in the authority of Yahweh asserted with the "self-
presentation formula" (*Selbstvorstellungsformel*).
Amos has only ironically parodied this form of
priestly Torah, as the statement which gives the

---

111. Cf. *BH*.

112. Initially, J. Begrich, "Die priesterliche Tora" in *Werden und
Wesen des Alten Testaments* (BZAW, 66; 1936), pp. 63–88. Cf.
further W. Zimmerli, "'Leben' und 'Tod' im Buche des Propheten
Ezechiel," *Gottes Offenbarung* (ThB 19; 1963), p. 185. But the
language and thought of Ezekiel is not without further consideration to be compared with the cultural world of Amos, even though
related thoughts do appear in Ezekiel. The conditional style in
Ezekiel 18:5–9 and the grounding of the argument in the declaratory judgment as a basis in Ezekiel 33:10–20 points to a quite different character to the "exhortation."

grounds (*Begründungssatz*) for his words at 4:4 f. shows:

"for so you love to do, O sons of Israel." (4:5c)

Priestly Torah in such places would use "Thus Yahweh loves to do" or a similar "declaratory formula."[113] In this manner Deutero-Isaiah genuinely takes up the form of the priestly divine decree when he grounds the summons to fearlessness in the declaration, "for I am your God!" (Isa. 41:8 ff.). Countless priestly cultic exhortations have their basis in the simple and yet so important statement, "for I am Yahweh (your God),"[114] which absolutely excludes all other motives. Further, Amos does not set forth *heilsgeschichte* as the basis of exhortations, such as we find at Exodus 23:9 and elsewhere. The priestly kind of exhortation and that exemplified in cult formulations does not, therefore, come into consideration as an actual prototype for the exhortations; only in 4:5b does Amos parody it.[115] But precisely this announcement, in its preamble,

113. Cf. G. von Rad, "Faith Reckoned as Righteousness," *Hexateuch* (cited above, note 39), pp. 125–30; R. Rendtorff, "Priesterliche Kulttheologie und prophetische Kultpolemik," *TLZ* 81 (1956): 339–42.

114. E.g., Lev. 18 f.; cf. W. Zimmerli, "Ich bin Jahwe," *Offenbarung* (cited above, note 112), pp. 11–40.

115. From this point it is easy to see a bold adoption and modification of the language customary in the cult, even in the section at 5:21–27, which has been designated as a "prophetic cult decree"; cf. E. Würthwein, "Kultpolemik" (cited above, note 34), pp. 115–31. In 4:5 f.; 5:4–6, 21–27, along with the cultic categories determined here by the theme, the plural form of address also is more reminiscent of cultic proclamation than of clan instruction, which uses the singular form throughout. With Amos, however, the address to Israel results from his commission (cf. 7:15b).

> Seek Bethel, and transgress,
> Gilgal, and transgress even more!

shows how Amos's irony is determined by his own characteristic mode of thought and speech, as we encounter it at 5:4, 6, 14 f. In each of these cases the consequence is described in the exhortation.

The other type of exhortation speech which cannot be considered as background for the form in Amos is that which developed from the "summons to national lament."[116] This type grounds the exhortation to some specified act of repentance in a reference to some crisis which has occurred. The reason cited in 5:5*b* could, indeed, be understood as a modification of this form insofar as the exhortation is grounded in a disaster which is announced rather than in one which has occurred; yet the distinctive features of the national lament are lacking in the imperatival clauses. Hence, even the statement which gives the grounds for his exhortation (*Begründungssatz*) is better viewed as a warning against pilgrimages,

> for Gilgal shall go to the gallows,
> and the house of God to the devil,

than as prophetic modification of the description of the result. The prohibition warns against the "snares of death."

Only 5:6*b* remains to be considered. Here the exhortation,

> Seek Yahweh and live! (5:6*a*)

116. Cf. H. W. Wolff, "Der Aufruf zur Volksklage," *ZAW* 76 (1964): 48–56, and e.g., Jer. 4:5–8; 6:26; Ezek. 21:17, etc.

is provided with a "lest" (*pen*) clause as a supplement, which, while indeed textually difficult, nevertheless means something like this:

> lest Joseph's house break out in fire
> which is not to be extinguished.[117]

This clause reminds us of the form of the admonition (*Ermahnung*) found in legal proceedings at the city gate when a suggestion for arbitration is made, in order to prevent incurring punishment.[118] Here the speakers are, as a rule, clan elders and heads of families; therefore, groups similar to those on whom responsibility for education in the clan was incumbent. Thus, such "lest" (*pen*) clauses frequently appear as modifications of the description of results also in wisdom exhortation speeches.

Love not sleep lest you become poor! (Prov. 20:13)

When your enemy falls, do not rejoice . . .
    lest Yahweh see it and be displeased. . . !

(Prov. 24:17 f.)

Reprove not a scoffer lest he hate you! (Prov. 9:8)

It is noteworthy that in all these cases the prohibition before the "lest" (*pen*) clause—as always in Amos—is formed with *'al* as the negative. In contrast, the cultically transmitted form of the apodictic exhortations prefers *lō'* as the negative (Exod. 20:3 ff.; 23:1 ff.).

117. On the problems of the text, cf. *BH* and V. Maag (cited above, note 51), pp. 26 f.
118. Cf. H. W. Wolff, *Hosea* (BKAT 14/1; 1961), pp. xv, 37 ff.; and H. J. Boecker, *Redeformen des Rechtslebens im Alten Testament* (WMANT, 14; 1964), pp. 120–23.

Instructive here is the comparison of two warning sayings (*Warnworte*) which are related in content:

A widow and an orphan you shall not (*lō'*) oppress!
(Exod. 22:21)

Do not (*'al*) disturb the boundary of a "widow,"[119]
and enter not (*'al*) the field of an orphan! (Prov. 23:10)

It must be concluded that in the exhortation speeches both formulations of apodictic law and formulations of language for instruction, employed in certain clans even in Amos's time, go back to the same linguistic form. At the same time, however, it must be said that ancient Israelite clan law developed differently in various branches of tradition. The sacral language of official priests and of those who made known the law (*Rechtskünder*) at the sanctuaries and at the great central festivals was somewhat different from that of the elders and heads of families who were teachers of the family. Both sorts of language did use forms that were related, like the exhortation sayings and prohibitions; but they differed noticeably in the way the forms were developed—on the one hand, with a preference for the description of the consequences, and on the other, with a preference for an authoritative basis (*Begründung*) cited.

Moreover, clan wisdom employed its own completely peculiar forms, as we observed them in the didactic questions, the "woe-cry," and the numerical sequence. The characteristic rhetorical forms of Amos are to be understood only if we seek his cultural background in this wisdom realm.

119. Cf. *BH*.

PART TWO:

Characteristic Themes

WE have not been able to discuss the form-critical problems without at the same time touching on questions of the contents (*Topik*) and thus indirectly of the themes (*Thematik*) of Amos. Now, in part summing up and in part going further, we want to examine here the actual contents of Amos's speeches to see which areas of Israelite life throw most light upon the man.

1. ISRAEL AND THE NATIONS

We begin with some negative observations which speak immediately against attempts to suppose that Amos is one who speaks officially for a central cult of the covenant and for the legal pronouncements coined there. Key words like "covenant" and "law" (*berît* and *tôrāh*)[120] appear in none of the speeches preserved for us. In contrast, both words appear repeatedly in Hosea who was Amos's contemporary and neighbor with regard to the locale of his public activity. But this is to be expected because Hosea was

---

120. *tôrāh* occurs only at 2:4, in the indictment against Judah, which does not stem from Amos; *berît*, only at 1:9 in the indictment against Edom, which likewise does not go back to Amos (in any case the word does not refer here to the divine covenant). For literary criticism, see note 86 above.

intensively occupied with the cultic traditions of Israel.[121] In the same way it is a fact that Amos himself never calls Yahweh "the God of Israel" or "your God,"[122] a point which distinguishes him again not only from Hosea (cf., for example, Hos. 4:6; 12:10; 13:4; 14:2) but significantly from the typical formularies of the so-called cult of the covenant. In addition, a rigorous literary-critical analysis shows that not only the Sinai tradition but also the tradition of the exodus from Egypt as a tradition about election is not found in Amos himself.[123]

Clearly Amos knew about the election of Israel (3:2) and, in the giving of the land, about Yahweh's special intervention against the strong Amorites on behalf of the weak (2:9). But this reminiscence is inserted solely to point out guilt and thereby to provide a basis for the message which puts Israel back among the pagan nations, just as is done in an unheard-of manner when Israel is included in the cycle of oracles against the nations (1:3–2:6 ff.) and when Israel is compared with the Ethiopians (9:7a). To this tendency also belongs the paralleling of Israel's exodus from Egypt with the exodus of the Philistines and of

121. Cf. Hosea 4:6; 6:7; 8:1, 12; and H. W. Wolff, *Hosea* (cited above, note 118), pp. xiv ff.

122. R. Smend (cited above, note 8), p. 415, has correctly shown this, without overlooking Amos 2:8.

123. On 3:1b, cf. now R. Smend, ibid., p. 409, note 25. Amos 2:10 is most probably also secondary, for, so far as the contents go, it belongs before 2:9; because of its traditional phrasings, it clearly departs from the original formulation in 2:9; it shifts into the form of direct address, whereas previously those indited appear only in the third person. The secondary character of 2:11 f. has been made clear by S. Lehming, "Erwägungen zu Amos" (cited above, note 26), pp. 146–51. Cf. also W. Schmidt (cited above, note 26). On 9:7b, see what follows.

the Syrians likewise under Yahweh (9:7*b*). Elsewhere, too, Amos knows much more that is positive about neighboring kingdoms (6:2!) and indirectly even about the great kingdoms of Assyria[124] and Egypt (3:9) than he does about Israel.

In his noncultic, critical comments about Israel and in his awareness of the fortunes and atrocities of many other peoples, does not Amos participate in a certain international culture which is more akin, in its parallels, to wisdom than to typical cultic thought? Admittedly, it is not the wisdom of the great courts. But do not the elders, when they wander with their herds, exchange experiences at oases and at meeting places for caravans? There they learn how Philistines sell slaves to Edom (1:6), that Ammonites rip open pregnant women in Gilead (1:13), and how Moabites deal with the corpse of an Edomite king (2:1).

Yet with these observations on the noncultic view of Israel which Amos holds and the classification of him in a broader international context, we have penetrated only to the edge of the themes of Amos. We are led on into the heart of the message charged to him concerning the end of Israel's particular history (8:2). On what does he base this message?

2. THE "RIGHT" WAY (*Das Gerade*)

A man can betray what his cultural home is with a single characteristic word. In Amos such a word appears at 3:10*a*:

They do not understand how to do what is *right*.

124. According to the Greek.

The word *nᵉkōḥāh*, used here for "right," never appears in covenant traditions or in legal literature.[125] In Amos, however, it fits in quite naturally in the speech where, along with the evils which Israel does, Amos once, by way of exception, mentions the positive element in her conduct which he misses. It is the term which occurs frequently in wisdom for what is "right."

> He who gives the right answer (*dᵉbārîm nᵉkōḥîm*)
> kisses the lips.   (Prov. 24:26)

In Proverbs 8:8 f. Wisdom calls:

All the words of my mouth are righteous;
  there is nothing twisted or crooked in them.
They are all straight (*nᵉkōḥîm*) to him who understands,
  and right for those who find knowledge (*da'at*).

Here the "straight" (or "right") is clarified as the opposite of the "twisted" and "crooked" in wisdom thought and as the object of discerning knowledge. Just as here, so also in Amos, the term *yāda'* ("know, understand") surfaces in the vocabulary:

> They do not *understand* how to do what is *right.*

Sirach 11:21 takes up the term in wisdom theology[126]:

---

125. S. Terrien, "Amos and Wisdom" (cited above, note 26), pp. 112 f., has correctly pointed to that as highly characteristic.
126. For the text, cf. R. Smend, *Sirach* (cited above, note 97), p. 109.

Do not be terrified by the actions of the godless!
   Trust Yahweh and wait for his light!
For it is right (*nkḥ*) in the eyes of Yahweh
   to enrich a poor man quite suddenly.

Here, too, there occurs something which is related to
the context in Amos. To the phrase "Do not be terrified" in the Sirach passage ('*al-ttmh*[127] = Greek *mē
thaumaze*) corresponds the call to Assyria and Egypt
in Amos 3 to gather on the mountains of Samaria in
order to see the "terror" (*meḥûmôt*, 3:9*b*) in her
midst. Here, too, as in Sirach, the concern is with the
"actions of the godless," which, however, are por-
trayed more precisely as "oppression," "violence,"
and "robbery" in 3:9*b*, 10*b*.[128] Finally, in Sirach the
"uprightness" of Yahweh is to make the poor rich,
while Amos threatens with collapse of their power
and possessions those who do not know what is *right*
and instead store up treasures by means of violent
deeds (3:10*b*, 11). In examining the vocabulary one
does not get the impression that the Sirach passage is
shaped by prophetic proclamation. Here and there a
theme not uncommon in wisdom is clustered around
the typical, major catchword found in wisdom literature: what is "right."

   In Isaiah the word appears at 30:10 in the contro-

---

127. According to R. Smend (ibid.), p. 108.

128. In addition, already in the early proverbial material (Prov.
15:16) '*ôṣār* ("store up," "treasure") and *meḥûmāh* ("tumult,"
"trouble") appear similarly, right alongside each other, just as in
the corresponding sayings in Amos 3:9*b*–10:

   Better is little with the fear of Yahweh
      than great *trouble* and *treasure* with it. (Prov. 15:16)
   . . . see the great *tumults* within her. . . .
   . . . those who *store up* violence . . . (Amos 3:9*b*–10)

versy with court (diplomatic) wisdom circles,[129] the representatives of which

> say to the seers, "See not!"
> and to those who have visions,
> "Prophesy not to us what is right ($n^e k\bar{o}h\hat{o}t$)!"

The very interesting question can be raised here whether the catchword "what is right" belongs to the language of the educated classes in court, or whether it is used in connection with the "seers," since Amos, indeed, is so addressed by Amaziah in 7:12 and is characterized as such in the superscription of his book.[130] The one heretofore unmentioned occurrence of "right" in preexilic texts[131] in 2 Samuel 15:3 argues primarily for the former sense, for there Absalom terms the words of a man seeking justice at court "good and right." Apparently the "right" means what is lawful in the wisdom language of the court as well as in the language of the clans. It is in this latter sense that Amos has taken it over.[132]

3. JUSTICE AND RIGHTEOUSNESS
(Rechtsordnung und Rechtverhalten)

. The most frequently repeated key words by which Amos measures the guilt of Israel are *mišpāṭ* (justice)

129. Cf. Isa. 29:14 and J. Fichtner (cited above, note 80), col. 80.

130. See below, p. 59. In Isaiah, too (28:7 ff.!) the *nebî'îm* (prophets) belong in the camp of the opponents, while Isaiah himself stands on the side of the "seers" (cf. with 30:10 both 1:1 and 2:1).

131. In postexilic texts it appears at Isa. 57:2; 59:14; 26:10.

132. According to H. Donner, "Die soziale Botschaft der Propheten im Lichte der Gesellschaftsordnung in Israel," *Oriens Antiquus* II (1963): 229–45, Amos 3:9 ff. is directed against "the principal Canaanite officialdom of Samaria" and against "typical Canaanite forms of economic oppression" (p. 236). Amos opposes this on the basis of the ideas from ancient Israelite clan justice.

and ṣedāqāh (righteousness).[133] They appear in pairs no less than three times.

(Woe to those),[134] who turn *justice* into wormwood
and cast *righteousness* to the ground. (Amos 5:7)

Let *justice* roll down like water,
righteousness like a steady stream. (5:24)

Do horses run on rocks?
Or does one plow the sea with the ox?[135]
But you have turned *justice* into poison,
and the fruit of *righteousness* into wormwood. (6:12)

In addition, mišpāṭ appears once more by itself:

Hate evil! Love good!
Enforce *justice* in the gate! (5:15)

Merely to observe in what rhetorical forms these terms occur is very illuminating. In 5:7 there is a saying which corresponds to the type of the "woe-cry" in clan wisdom;[136] in 6:12 the pair of terms is bound up with characteristic wisdom didactic questions;[137] in 5:15 the wisdom type of exhortation speech[138] appears, and in addition, in terms of content, justice is

133. For the meaning of the word and for literature, cf. H. W. Wolff, *Hosea* (cited above, note 118), on Hosea 2:21.
134. For the text, see above, p. 18.
135. For the text, see above, p. 11.
136. See above, pp. 18 f. The 'asrê-cry in Psalm 106:3 forms an exact counterpart (see above, p. 25):
Blessed are those who observe mišpāṭ,
who do ṣedāqāh at all times.
137. See above, pp. 11 ff.
138. See above, pp. 44 ff.

appealed to as the task entrusted to the clan elders in the gate.

But how is the occurrence at 5:24 to be explained? Does it not appear here in connection with the "prophetic cult decree" of 5:21–23?[139] Does not this oracle, at least, then belong to the typical cultic manner of speech? Through a more detailed examination one must, for several reasons, answer these questions in the negative.

First it seems probable to us, in light of the parody on the priestly exhortation speech at 4:4 f.,[140] that in this abrupt statement which rejects Israel's feasts and offerings (vv. 21–23) Amos falls into the function and rhetorical form of a speaker imparting a cult decree as authorized agent of his God, only in order to announce the *opposite* of what was normally expected in the cult. Thus the exceptional use of specifically cultic terminology in vv. 21–23 is understandable. Further, we have seen that the direct continuation in vv. 25 f. takes up the style of didactic questions which in other cases in Amos corresponds to wisdom language.[141] The sentence at v. 24 itself, with its particular mode of comparison (". . . like waters, . . . like an ever-flowing stream") shows a feature characteristic of the wisdom sentence, as we have already often found it in Amos.[142]

It is decisive that in the whole Pentateuch and in the formulas handed down there, similar parallel

139. Cf. E. Würthwein, "Kultpolemik" (cited above, note 34), and on that see above, note 115.
140. See above, pp. 49 f.
141. See above, pp. 11 ff.
142. See above, p. 15.

formulations about justice and righteousness never appear as they do in Amos.[143] However, they are found repeatedly in wisdom material.

> Better is a little with *righteousness*
> than great revenues without *justice*. (Prov. 16:8)

That here, too, in terms of content, we are completely in the area of Amos's interests is evident from the way in which he accuses the merchants who

> diminish the measure,
> but increase the weights
> in order to deceive with false balances. (Amos 8:5)

The choice of words shows the proximity to the wisdom tradition. Cf. Proverbs 16:11:

> Scales and balances of justice ($m\bar{o}'zn\hat{e}\ mi\check{s}p\bar{a}t$) are the Lord's,
> all the weights in the bag are his work.

The same word as in Amos ($m\bar{o}'zn\hat{e}\ mirm\bar{a}h$) is used at Proverbs 20:23:

> A double standard in weights is an abomination to Yahweh,
> and a deceitful balance is not good.

143. Deuteronomy 33:21 speaks of *Yahweh's* justice and righteousness, as occasionally do other, mostly later, texts: cf. Ps. 36:7; 99:4; Jer. 9:23; Isa. 5:16; 33:5. Genesis 18:19 mentions as a secondary ingredient in the Yahwistic context (cf. Martin Noth, *A History of Pentateuchal Traditions* [*Überlieferungsgeschichte des Pentateuchs*], trans. Bernhard W. Anderson [Englewood Cliffs, N.J.: Prentice-Hall, 1972], p. 239) the formulalike "doing righteousness and justice," just as Ezekiel in a stereotyped way later describes the "righteous" with this formula (Ezek. 18:5, 19, 21, 27; 33:14, 16, 19; 45:9). For Lev. 19:15 and Deut. 16:18–20, see below, pp. 65 ff.

Likewise it is said in the old collection at Proverbs 11:1:

> A false balance is an abomination to the Lord,
>   but a full weight (finds) his pleasure.[144]

It is noteworthy that the whole pentateuchal tradition speaks of weights only in Leviticus 19, a chapter which otherwise groups in apodictic style traditions of the ancient clans. In Leviticus, however, in contrast to Amos and to Proverbs, the phrase is *mō'znê-ṣedeq*, and the instruction, which appears in the plural imperative style—corresponding to religious formularies—concludes with "I am Yahweh. . . ."

The connection between Amos and the wisdom tradition becomes especially clear when we look at the context of the negative "cult decree" (in which Amos 5:24 stands) in Proverbs 21:3:

> Do justice and righteousness,
>   that is more pleasing to Yahweh than sacrifice.

Further in a statement from the oldest proverbial collection (Prov. 15:8):

> The sacrifice of the wicked is an abomination to Yahweh,
>   but the prayer of the upright (finds) his pleasure.

Proverbs 21:27 shows that the theme is not at all rare in wisdom.

> The sacrifice of the wicked is an abomination,
>   above all, when he brings it with evil intent.

144. Cf. also Prov. 20:10.

It is certainly no accident that the late collections designate the instructive content of proverbial wisdom as *ṣedeq ûmišpāṭ* (Prov. 1:3; 2:9).

Besides these parallels of wisdom proverbs to the statements of Amos, which lead to the conclusion that they have a common origin in the clan wisdom of the Israelite tribes, there is still one more important correspondence. It is that group of texts which designate "justice and righteousness" as the proper business of the king: 2 Samuel 8:15; 1 Kings 10:9; Psalm 72:1; Isaiah 9:6; Jeremiah 22:3, 15; 33:15. It is clear that this theme was a chief objective also in royal education and instruction, indeed the foundation, the "pedestal for the throne" of the regent.[145] What *maat* was in the wisdom of Egypt and thus in the education of princes and officials, the court wisdom of Davidic Jerusalem—in taking up the fundamentals of ancient Israelite clan education—called "justice and righteousness." On the basis of Isaiah's proximity to this coinage from Israelite wisdom, use of this pair of words at Isaiah 5:7 and 28:17 is understandable.

Thus it may be clearly seen that the theme "justice and righteousness," as it is repeated in Amos's proverbial material and is elaborated in his own way, strongly warns against finding the prophet's provenance in a central covenant cult marked by "covenant" and "law." Conversely, the same theme warns against comparing too hastily his rhetorical forms

145. Cf. H. Brunner, "Gerechtigkeit als Fundament des Thrones," *VT* 8 (1958): 426–28; on Isa. 9:6, cf. H. W. Wolff, *Frieden ohne Ende* (BSt 35; 1962), p. 72.

and subjects of proclamation with liturgical formularies, as they were shaped in the complex of the pentateuchal Sinai traditions.

To conclude this section and in order to gain a clearer picture of the relationship of clan wisdom to the cultus of the central sanctuaries, we turn to two passages in the Pentateuch in which not *mišpāṭ* and *ṣedāqāh* but *mišpāṭ* and *ṣedeq* appear in a way that is somewhat comparable to Amos and yet is very different. First to be considered is Leviticus 19:15:

You shall do no injustice in judgment (*mišpāṭ*)!
You shall not be partial to the poor!
You shall not defer to the great!
With righteousness (*ṣedeq*) shall you judge your neighbor!

This series of imperatives, introduced with a plural superscription in 15*a*, is continued in verse 16 with two further instructions, and concludes with "I am Yahweh." Here in Leviticus 19, apparently, there had been inserted a short series of commands in apodictic formulation which regulates "right behavior in the legal community 'in the gate.' "[146] It addresses not only the judges but, as especially verse 16 and even more clearly the following series in verses 17 f. shows, all Israelites, with regard to their behavior to other members of the community. It is quite clear here that the concern is with the ordering of communal life in the clan. It is not astonishing, therefore, that the statements agree in substance to a large extent with

146. Cf. M. Noth, *Leviticus*, trans. J. E. Anderson (The Old Testament Library; Philadelphia: Westminster, 1965), p. 141.

maxims that appear in a different formulation in proverbs as the traditional material of clan wisdom.[147] Apart from the great cultic framework of the Holiness Code (cf. 19:1 f.) and the authorizing conclusion using "I am Yahweh," the striking difference is the use of *mišpāṭ* and *ṣedeq*. Here in Leviticus 19 *mišpāṭ* appears only in the superscription as an encompassing catchword for the rules elucidated for the law court in what follows; *ṣedeq* appears later simply for the legal and communal behavior of the individual toward his neighbor. These sentences, elevated to apodictic covenant law, are not aware of a parallelism of "justice" and "righteousness" as we found it in both Amos and the clan wisdom of the proverbs. That shows us again that the great legal collections and religious documents of all Israel have taken up into themselves forms of ancient Israelite clan wisdom. Besides that, however, the will of Yahweh, at least within individual clans, was handed down orally until the time of Amos in another manner, namely, as wisdom. It is from this line of tradition that Amos is to be understood.[148]

This view is confirmed by Deuteronomy 16:18–20, where the concern is with "worldly organs of arbitration and settlement" in the "local government of the

147. Cf. Prov. 17:15; 18:5; 24:23; 28:21; and see Feucht (cited above, note 107), p. 109.
148. This must be said against the thesis of Henning Graf Reventlow, *Das Heiligkeitsgesetz formgeschichtlich untersucht* (WMANT, 6; 1961), according to which "the sitz im leben of the Israelite covenant festival" is "the underlying principle for the forms of the Holiness Code in particulars as well as on the whole" (p. 30). From such a one-sided view there must follow—among other things—the untenable thesis that Amos had been an official of the covenant cult cultus (see above, p. 3).

clan settlements of the tribes."[149] In accord with circumstances in the seventh century, *mišpaṭ ṣedeq*, i.e., proper administration of justice, was enjoined on the judges in general, and in particular they were warned against infraction of *mišpāṭ* as justice through partiality and bribery. By no means unimportant is the note that "bribery blinds the eyes of the wise" (v. 19). The catchword *ḥᵃkāmîm* indicates in the framework of the Deuteronomistic regulations that here the ones accountable for the administration of justice are addressed as the "wise." As in Leviticus 19:15 with the allusion to the "poor" (*dal*),[150] so also Deuteronomy 16:19, with the theme "bribery," is reminiscent of Amos (5:12). Both texts confirm, however, that the great cultic formularies mention "justice and righteousness" only where they actually give certain regulations for life of the clans. They do it not without demonstrably significant modifications, which show that Amos belongs on the side of ancient Israelite clan wisdom which was transmitted orally.

4. INDIVIDUAL THEMES

(a) The observations concerning the originality of the exhortation speech in Amos lead to the conviction that he favored certain *antithetical word-pairs* which were customary not in the exalted style of religious address but in family instruction. We think of the contrast between "good" and "evil" and between "love" and "hate"—as we met it in 5:14 f. In

149. Cf. F. Horst, *Gottes Recht* (cited above, note 57), pp. 129 f.
150. See above, p. 65 and below, pp. 70 ff.

addition, however, we must consider isolated cases as in the question at 6:2*b*:

> Are you better than that kingdom?

or in the woe-cry collection at 6:3:

> who imagine the evil day is far off,

or at 5:10:

They hate him who reproves in the gate,
  and they abhor him who makes a full declaration.

Even a quick glance into the concordance is sufficient to show that the antithetical word-pairs mentioned here are nowhere so favored as in proverbial wisdom and in the realm of Old Testament scripture related to it.

Do not they err who plan evil?
  Loyalty and faithfulness belong to those who plan good.
                                                        (Prov. 14:22)

Men of evil manner[151] do not understand justice,
  but those who seek the Lord understand everything.
Better is a poor man who walks in his integrity
  than one who goes a perverse path and is thereby rich.
                                                        (Prov. 28:5–6)

How such a statement reminds us of Amos! The contrast good-evil, as in Amos 5:15, is elucidated by the contrast of evil and justice. As in Amos 5:4, 6, 14 the quest for the good stands parallel to the seeking of

151. Cf. Gemser (cited above, note 41), in loc.

Yahweh. And the comparison of the innocent poor with the perverse rich corresponds precisely to the social criticism of the prophet (2:6 f.; 5:10 f.; 8:4 f.; etc.)! The question about the "good"[152] as the *leit-motif* of clan wisdom leads to the favorite form of the *ṭôb . . . min* proverbs, to which Proverbs 15:17 also belongs:

> Better is a dinner of herbs with love
> than of a fatted ox with hate.

By this type of comparison speech the question in 6:2*b* introduced above can also be understood. Even the reference to the "evil day" (Amos 6:3)[153] is familiar as a term from proverbs. Thus it appears in 16:4,

> Yahweh has made everything for its purpose,
> even the wicked for the evil day.

The contrast of love and hate—concerning which Proverbs 15:17 offered an example above—is nowhere so frequent as in proverbial material. From the older stock may further be added Proverbs 12:1:

---

152. Cf. U. Skladny (cited above, note 46), p. 36, on the problem concerning whether there is to be considered only "what is good for man" (W. Zimmerli, *ZAW* 51 [1933], pp. 192 ff. on Eccles. 6:12) or (at the same time) "what is good in the eyes of Yahweh" (cf. Prov. 15:16; 16:7 f.; 19:1; and especially 20:23 where *lō'-ṭôb* is explained as *tō'abat-YHWH*). Here is to be considered also the theme of the Joseph story in the Elohistic source (Gen. 50:20):
> What you have done against me as evil
> God has worked toward good.
On this see G. von Rad, "The Joseph Narrative and Ancient Wisdom," *Hexateuch* (cited above, note 39), pp. 296 ff.

153. Cf. also Ps. 41:2 and above, p. 26!

Whoever loves discipline loves knowledge,
   but he who hates reproof (*tôkaḥat*) is stupid.

Beside the contrast of love and hate in the exhortation saying at Amos 5:15, we should especially recall here 5:10 where Amos places under the "woe-cry" those "who hate him who reproves (*môkîaḥ*) in the gate." Cf. Proverbs 13:24:

He who spares the rod hates his son,
   but he who loves him is concerned with discipline.

Precisely such a proverb shows it is educative wisdom, formed and nurtured in the family, which had special preference for the topics treated here.[154] This wisdom found in the clan is similar to Amos (cf. 5:10 f., 14 f.) in that it calls for decision between love-with-discipline and hate-for-reproof as related to the choice between life and death.

Severe discipline comes upon him who forsakes the way,
   he who hates reproof will die. (Prov. 15:10)

What is new with Amos is that it is Israel's life as a whole that is at stake.

(b) Among the themes repeated most frequently by Amos belongs his concern for *the poor and needy*. The comparison between the proportionately rare occurrence of words for the "helpless" (*dal*) in Exodus

154. Further examples of hate and love are found at Proverbs 1:22; 9:8; 19:7 f. Can it be an accident that a comparable antithetical use of "love" and "hate" appears in the legal corpus only where the traditional material of the overall legal community of the clan is dealt with, namely Leviticus 19:17 f.?

23:3; Leviticus 19:15, the "poor" (*'ebyôn*) in Exodus 23:6, 11, or the "afflicted" (*'ānî*) in Exodus 22:24; Leviticus 19:10; 23:22, and their disproportionate frequency in the proverbial material is striking in itself. More important, however, is the way in which they appear: in the legal material the terms appear only separately from time to time, but in wisdom the references to those in want employ the terms in pairs throughout—precisely as in Amos.

Amos mentions the "helpless" (*dal*) in 2:7; 4:1; 5:11; 8:6; the "poor" (*'ebyôn*) in 2:6; 4:1; 5:12; 8:4, 6; the "oppressed" (*'ānî*) in 2:7[155] and 8:4. It is especially to be noted that twice the parallel to "the righteous" is "the needy" (2:6; 5:12). Amos 2:7 speaks of those

> who trample the head of the helpless,
> who deny[156] justice to the afflicted.

Here, Proverbs 22:22 is, above all, to be compared:

> Do not rob the helpless, because he is helpless!
> And do not crush the afflicted in the gate!

In demonstrating guilt, Amos obviously has in mind such a warning saying found in the ethics of the clan, as is shown not only by the parallel designation for the oppressed, but also by the situation "in the gate" as the place for administration of justice in the clan (cf. Amos 5:10, 12, 15). Highly interesting is the reason given in the first half-verse (Prov. 22:22*a*):

155. On *'anāwîm* as the plural of *'ānî*, cf. L. Delekat, "Zum hebräischen Wörterbuch," *VT* 14 (1964): 46.
156. For the text, see above, p. 18.

Do not rob the helpless, because he is helpless (*kî dal-hû'*)!

Amos argues in exactly the same way when in the first two visions (7:2, 5) he sees Israel exposed to the threat by Yahweh:

> Oh Lord Yahweh, forgive, I beseech thee!
> How can Jacob stand?
> For he is small (*kî qāton hû'*).

He does not draw attention to election, or to Yahweh's mercy; he does not bring up any of the reproaches customary in the great cultus. Rather he employs this simple wisdom allusion to the defenselessness of the perplexed.

Twice Amos sets the helpless and the poor in parallelism: at 4:1 he characterizes the women of Samaria as those

> who oppress the helpless,
> who crush the poor.

In 8:6 he designates as the goal of the greedy:

> to buy the helpless for silver
> and the poor for a pair of sandals.

The same parallelism appears at Proverbs 14:31:

> He who oppresses the helpless insults his Creator.
> But he who is merciful to the poor honors him.

As in Amos 4:1, here, too, the reference is to "oppressing" the helpless, and even the term "merciful" (*ḥnn*) is not strange to the language of Amos (5:15*b*, ". . . be gracious").

Most abundant are the parallels to the word-pair "poor-oppressed," occurring in Amos 8:4:

Hear this, you who trample upon the poor,
> who bring to an end the helpless of the land.[157]

First there is to be mentioned, at the climax of "The Words of Agur" (Prov. 30:14), the reference to the generation "whose teeth are swords and whose teeth are knives,"

> to devour the oppressed from off the earth,
> and the poor from the "arable land."[158]

Likewise there is attributed to the "wisdom of the people of the east" (1 Kings 5:10; English 4:30) the admonition from "The Sayings of Lemuel" which at Proverbs 31:8 f. reads:

> Open your mouth for the dumb,
> for the rights of all who are desolate!
> Open your mouth, judge in righteousness!
> Maintain justice for the helpless and the poor!

From such shaping of the tradition about God's will, Amos diagnoses the guilt of Israel,[159] even though the "oppressed" belong also under the theme of the *'ašrê*-cries (blessing-cries).[160]

---

157. L. Delekat (cited above, note 155), p. 47, translates "the destitute in the land."

158. Cf. *BH* and G. Sauer (cited above, note 85), p. 103.

159. Also in Proverbs 31:20 the parallel *'ānî-'ebyôn* occurs once again—there is connection with the ideal housewife:
> She opens her hand to the helpless,
> and reaches out her hands to the poor.

160. Prov. 14:21. Singly the terms occur in a corresponding theme in Proverbs 3:34; 15:15; 16:19; 19:17; 21:13; 22:9, 16; 28:3, 8, 11, 15; 29:14. Even the threat is not lacking, as Proverbs 15:25 shows:
> Yahweh tears down the house of the proud,
> but he maintains the widow's boundaries.
Cf. Amos 3:15; 5:11; 6:8 with 2:6.

(c) Just as the member of the clan is educated to
show regard for the poor, so on the other hand he is
warned against *an extravagant life*. Amos turns repeatedly against those who indulge in wine to
excess—from the women of Samaria who say to their
husbands,

> "Bring that we may drink!" (4:1),

to those circles of leaders

> who drink wine from bowls
>   and anoint themselves with the finest oil. (6:6)

Cf. also 2:8 and 5:11!

We have no evidence for the claim that at the
great central festivals of Israel and in the formularies
connected with them the theme of sumptuousness
ever played a significant role. But surely there were,
even beyond the time of Amos, clan units who in a
most critical way opposed the gluttonous life of the
settled land, as the example of the Rechabites at
Jeremiah 35:6 most directly shows. Clan wisdom had
often demonstrably taken up this theme. In connection with the "woe-cry," we have only to recall Proverbs 23:29 ff.[161] Proverbs 21:17 warns simultaneously
against wine and oil, the same way we found them
alongside each other in Amos 6:6:

He who loves pleasure will be a poor man,
    he who loves wine and oil will not become rich.

> (Prov. 21:17)

161. See above, p. 24.

Bound up precisely with that theme of care for the afflicted, outlined above, is the warning against wine in a proverb associated with the "wisdom of the people of the east," namely, "The Words of Lemuel," and thus not belonging to the great court wisdom:

It is not fitting for a king to drink wine,
 or for a prince to desire strong drink,
lest he drink and forget the decrees
 and pervert the justice of all the afflicted. (Prov. 31:4 f.)

The antithetical "woe-blessed" cry in Ecclesiastes 10:16 f. belongs here too.[162] How lively the interest was in the theme of the enjoyment of wine—even for the wisdom woe-cries—is shown also at Isaiah 5:11 f., 22 f.[163]

The wisdom of the old proverbial collections in Israel can be explained as an attempt "to anchor faith in the guidance of Yahweh even in the realm of everyday human social life."[164] In its own way it is agitated very much in the same way as the prohibitions of apodictic law and certain areas of the so-called covenantal preaching in the Book of the Covenant and in Leviticus 18 f. The peculiarities of theme, like those of linguistic form, do not point to the same (cultic) tradition of ancient Israelite legal proclamation. Rather they show that the clans and families, too, in their own way and with their peculiar accentuation of themes, still carried on the divine justice of ancient Israel from generation to

162. On this, see above, p. 29.
163. See above, p. 31.
164. Thus U. Skladny (cited above, note 46), p. 95.

generation. Research in recent decades has not completely escaped the danger of stressing too strongly texts like Deuteronomy 31:9–13.[165] Thus scholarship has not sufficiently reckoned with the breadth and variety of the special traditions in at least some clans of Israel for an understanding of many phenomena in the life of Israel's monarchical period. For that reason also, research has fallen into the temptation to interpret the prophet Amos more on the basis of a general cultic system than on the basis of the particularity of Israelite clan life, established clearly enough through the themes he treats. To be sure, Amos was not aware of the theme, developed in later wisdom, of the fear of God as the ultimate characteristic of wisdom,[166] but it is no accident that he compared the urgency of his prophetic office to the inevitable "fear" at the roar of a lion. By doing so, he borrowed a concept which "apparently had been avoided in priestly circles" and which shows "that essential concepts of Judaic-Israelite piety had not developed in the cultic and priestly traditions, but had been given their character in other strata of the people's life."[167]

165. Cf. Feucht (cited above, note 107), p. 80.
166. Prov. 1:7, 29; 2:5, etc. With Amos 3:9 ff.; 5:14 f., cf. especially Prov. 14:27; 15:16; 16:6 (8:13); further, Amos 3:8.
167. So Siegfried Plath, *Furcht Gottes—Der Begriff* yr' *im Alten Testament* (Arbeiten zur Theologie, 2, 2; Stuttgart: Calwer Verlag, and East Berlin: Evangelische Verlagsanstalt, 1962), p. 122.

PART THREE:

Peripheral Problems

1. TEKOA

Amos came from Tekoa. It has often been pointed out that that place belongs to the system of border fortifications which stem from the time of Rehoboam or perhaps from a somewhat later period (cf. 2 Chron. 11:6).[168] At any rate when Amos the shepherd moved from Tekoa eastward and southward, he came into contact with Edomites and other "people of the east," with whom he could exchange experiences and knowledge, pieces of news, and old proverbial material.[169] Perhaps it is no accident that, according to 2 Samuel 14:2, Joab had brought to the Jerusalem court a "wise woman" precisely from Tekoa, which lay ten miles to the south. She understood how to introduce a legal case (vv. 6 f.); how, by use of an analogy from nature, to elevate it to the level of a principle, especially with regard to the rights of an outcast (v. 14);

168. On the problem of the age of the lists incorporated in the Chronicler's work, cf. M. Noth, *Überlieferungsgeschichtliche Studien I* (Tübingen: Max Niemeyer, ³1967), p. 140 f.; K. Galling, *Die Bücher der Chronik* (ATD 12; 1954), pp. 104 f.; and W. Randolph, *Chronikbücher* (HAT I, 21; 1955), pp. 228 f.

169. On the "wisdom of the people of the east," in distinction to the court "wisdom of Egypt" (according to 1 Kings 5:10 ff. [English, 4:30 ff.]), see above, p. 37.

and how at the end to come to the choice between "good and evil" (v. 17).[170] Such a "wise woman," "whose husband is known in the gates, when he sits among the elders of the land" (Prov. 31:23), is by no means to be found everywhere, even if one should not overlook the only related case in 2 Samuel 20:16 ff.

In any case, Amos challenges us to the assumption that ancient Israelite wisdom, with its peculiar forms and themes, was intensively cultivated in Tekoa. What came to expression "in the gate" there probably had almost as much relationship with the wisdom of the neighboring "people of the east" as it had with the court wisdom of Jerusalem and the cultic traditions of the central sanctuary. It is an unsolved problem of research, on the one hand, to distinguish clan wisdom, cultivated "in the gate" of cities as well as at the oasis meeting places of shepherds, from the court wisdom of the schools for princes and officials of the monarchs; and on the other hand, to investigate the influence on the legal pronouncements used in the cult centers from the rhetorical forms of clan wisdom and their modification. Amos not only compels us to such an investigation; he also provides no inconsiderable material for the task.

2. THE HOUSE OF ISAAC

Amos is the only prophet who speaks of the "house of Isaac" in parallel to "Israel" (7:16) and of the "high places of Isaac" in parallel to the "sanctuaries of Israel" (7:9). Even in the rest of the Old Testament

170. See above, pp. 59 f.

too this sort of expression is quite unusual. Any attempt at explanation surely may not disregard the other unique piece of evidence in the prophetic literature, namely, that only Amos alludes to the sanctuary at Beer-sheba (5:5; 8:14); for ever since Genesis 26:23, 25, 33; 46:1–4 Beer-sheba had been bound up with the Isaac tradition. This curious double observation is above all noteworthy because, on the one hand, Amos always speaks of Isaac only in clear parallels to the Northern Kingdom of Israel and also always mentions Beer-sheba in the same breath with northern sanctuaries; however, on the other hand, Beer-sheba, as an oasis in the Negeb, itself lies deep in the south of Judah.

As a rule, the problem has been explained in the following manner: Beer-sheba is said to have been a place of pilgrimage for northern Israelites, and the Isaac tradition to have been cultivated particularly in the Joseph tribes.[171] With this explanation, however, the question remains open why only Amos spoke of Isaac (and Beer-sheba) and not, for example, Hosea, who in his origins was bound up much more closely with the Northern Kingdom. Thus the idea could arise that one must reckon with the pentateuchal tradition about Isaac as the father of Jacob and Esau, and thus of Israelites as well as of Edomites (Gen. 25:29 f.).[172] Amos of Tekoa, who perhaps also

---

171. Cf. W. Zimmerli, *Geschichte und Tradition von Beer-Seba im Alten Testament* (Giessen: Töpelmann, 1932), and A. Jepsen, "Zur Überlieferungsgeschichte der Vätergestalten," *Wissenschaftliche Zeitschrift* (Leipzig) 3 (1953/54): 144 f.; A. Weiser, *Das Buch der zwölf Kleinen Propheten* (ATD 24; 41963), p. 185.

172. So S. Terrien (cited above, note 26), pp. 113 f.

sought out the oasis at Beer-sheba often, may with the people of his clan have regarded as a brother nation the neighboring seminomads who lived a similar kind of life (Num. 20:14; Deut. 23:8). Thus, he may also have shared in the famous "wisdom of the Edomites."[173] Only with great caution may one have recourse to such conjectures as hypotheses. For the present textual form in Amos has in mind only the Northern Kingdom of Israel. Still, a completely satisfactory solution will have to reckon with Amos's unique linguistic usage as regards "Isaac," together with the evidence of his geographical and cultural background.

3. AMOS AND ISAIAH

For some time a definite relationship of Isaiah with Amos has been recognized.[174] Recently the thesis has even been advocated: "It is quite certain that Isaiah was acquainted with Amos's rhetoric, whether he always imitated it consciously or not; often he stands thematically in his footsteps, although linguistically, as well as theologically, he never takes over his statements unchanged."[175] The documentation for this thesis is rather sparse in many places because the author is actually concerned with Isaiah's relationship to wisdom,[176] and yet, strangely enough, the thought never occurs to him that the sayings of Amos could also be determined by the rhetorical forms and themes

173. On this, see above, note 91.
174. Cf. R. Fey (cited above, note 47), pp. 7 f.
175. Ibid., p. 147.
176. In connection, above all, with the work of J. Fichtner (cited above, note 80); cf. R. Fey (ibid.), p. 8 and elsewhere.

of wisdom. In view of our inquiries into the "woe-cries" in Amos[177] this lack of insight is astonishing, especially in the comparison of Isaiah 5:11–13 with Amos 6:1–7.[178] At the least, there is much in the form and content of Isaiah which, just as in Amos, is to be understood directly from the related wisdom traditions.

I illustrate that with only one example, from Isaiah 5:20, 23:

> [20] Woe to those who call evil good and good evil,
>   who put darkness for light and light for darkness,
>   who put bitter for sweet and sweet for bitter!
> [23] . . . who acquit the guilty for a bribe,
>   and deprive the *innocent* of his *right*! (RSV)

Isaiah is said to "have formulated" his proverb at 5:20, 23 "with reference to" Amos 5:7, 10, 12b.[179] What is the basis for this conjectured dependence? First it is said, "no other Isaianic occurrence of *ṣᵉdā-qāh* stands conceptually so close to Amos as this one."[180] What is meant is the statement at Isaiah 5:23b:

> The justice of "the righteous"[181] they deny him.

It is said to be derived from Amos 5:7b,

---

177. Above, pp. 17 ff.
178. With this comparison R. Fey opens his investigation (cited above, note 47), pp. 9 ff.
179. Ibid., p. 58.
180. Ibid., p. 57.
181. Cf. *BH* (*ṣidqat ṣāddîq*).

They cast down righteousness to the earth,

and from Amos 5:12*b*,

who afflict the righteous.

Isaiah's word usage is said to go beyond Amos only insofar as for him righteousness "cloaks the man in a protective way and can be removed from him in unfair legal proceedings."[182] For Amos 5:7 we have already established that the parallel sayings about justice and righteousness are to be explained from the tradition of clan wisdom.[183] The actual Isaianic formulation "justice of the righteous" is to be understood neither on the basis of the speeches of Amos nor on the basis of tradition transmitted to him. Rather it is to be explained directly by another type of rhetoric, from wisdom, which occurs in Proverbs 11:5, 6. The *ṣidqat ṣāddîq* of Isaiah (5:23) corresponds precisely to *ṣidqat tāmîm* in Proverbs 11:5 and *ṣidqat ʾyᵉsārîm* in 11:6.

⁵ The *righteousness of the blameless* keeps straight his way,
    but the wicked falls by his own wickedness.
⁶ The *righteousness of the upright* saves them,
    but by their[184] lust the unfaithful are taken captive.

For here too the idea is at home that such righteousness is itself protective power. Therefore Isaiah, in

182. Ibid., p. 58.
183. See above, pp. 59 ff.
184. *BH.*

his word usage and in his way of looking at things, is to be understood here directly on the basis of wisdom, just as Amos is for his part.

Next, the reference to bribery in Isaiah 5:23 is said to go back to Amos 5:12*b*. In Isaiah 5:23 the concern is for "those who acquit the guilty for a bribe"; Amos (5:12*b*) criticizes those who "accept a bribe." If one looks at the actual formulations more closely, the dependence of Isaiah on Amos becomes quite questionable here too. For the theme "acquit the guilty" (*maṣdîq rāšāʿ*) is at Proverbs 17:15 a literally analogous wisdom theme:

> He who acquits the guilty and he who condemns the
> righteous—
>   both are an abomination to Yahweh.

In addition, "bribery" in Isaiah is *šōḥad*; in Amos, on the contrary, it is *kōper*. Isaiah uses the same word *šōḥad* also in 1:23 where the concern is with court officials. It belongs to the language of the court (cf. 2 Kings 16:8). Amos, on the contrary, speaks the language which is at home "in the gate" (cf. Amos 5:10) of the clan settlement (cf. Exod. 21:30). The observation of such linguistic variants could perhaps serve as the starting point for the necessary distinction between clan wisdom and court wisdom. Proverbs in which both traditions flow together use both words.[185]

Finally, it is said that the four antithetical pairs in Isaiah 5:20 expand "a single word of Amos," namely, the verb "turn," "the *hpk* of Amos 5:7*a* (and

185. *šōḥad* in 6:35; 17:8, 23; 21:14; *kōper* in 6:35; 13:8; 21:18.

6:12*b*?).''[186] In particular, Isaiah is said to have commented upon this term from Amos by using other words of Amos. Even if one can seriously consider that Isaiah was acquainted with Amos's proclamation of judgment,[187] it surely implies a misunderstanding of Isaiah's manner of proclamation to regard him in this way as a commentator on earlier prophetic preaching. The turning of justice into poison (Amos 5:7*a*) is said to be interpreted by Amos 5:14 f.[188] in the "woe-cry" at Isaiah 5:20,

> Woe to those who call evil good and good evil.

Against this, we have seen that the antithetical pair "good-evil" belongs generally to the themes of proverbial wisdom material[189]—in the court as well as in the clan. The pair "light-darkness" is said to be reminiscent of Amos 5:18–20; however, in fact, Isaiah 5:20 and Amos 5:18 ff., as "woe-cries," must be seen as derived from wisdom. It is in the linguistic realm of wisdom that the contrast of "light-darkness," like that of "good-evil," also belonged from early times.[190] The same is true for the pair "sweet-bitter" which Isaiah 5:20 presents third in its antithetical pairs. It is said to have originated from Amos's comparison with the wormwood in 5:7 (6:12), although it is much better explained from the general wisdom dis-

186. R. Fey (cited above, note 47), p. 58.
187. On Isa. 9:7, cf. ibid., p. 104.
188. Ibid., p. 58.
189. See above, pp. 67 ff.
190. Even if the literary examples stem from a later period; cf. Prov. 2:13; Job 12:22; 18:18; 24:13–17; Eccles. 2:13.

position toward the formation of such antithetical pairs. This is especially clear from Proverbs 27:7.

Almost all comparisons which are made between the words of Isaiah and of Amos must be similarly investigated. The question of the dependence of the Jerusalemite Isaiah on the prophet from Tekoa can be satisfactorily explained only when one considers the direct connection of both with the wisdom tradition and thereby, at the same time, reckons with a distinction between a Jerusalem-court version of wisdom and special forms of the clans. Besides the mutuality of the "woe-cries" and many individual themes, it would be well to pay attention to the peculiarity, e.g., of the tradition of the numerical sequence in Amos and certain didactic analogies.

4. WISDOM AND THE PROCLAMATION OF JUDGMENT

In his proclamation Amos introduces "profane," noncultic language and the way of thinking found in clan wisdom[191] *only* in his linguistic framework and in demonstrating guilt. That must once again be emphasized strongly. The totality and the particulars of his message cannot be deduced in this way, from these backgrounds. His message is one of the inevitable end of Israel (Amos 8:2 and, accordingly, at the conclusion of almost every single prophetic unit).[192] Of course, wisdom material too had always pointed out consequences and, especially with its "woe- and blessing-cries," intended to give instruction for dis-

191. Cf. G. von Rad, *Old Testament Theology*, vol. 1 (cited above, note 92), pp. 435 ff.
192. See above, p. 5.

tinguishing the way of life from the snares of death.[193] But these sayings consistently applied to the individual in Israel. Something similar must be said about cultic curses, in any case about the ancient curse dodecalogue, which is to be explained form-critically from the "woe-cries."[194] Here individuals are mentioned from time to time who were separated from the covenant community in order that all Israel might remain secure in the covenant. Only in the aftermath of prophetic preaching, in Deuteronomy 28 is all Israel shoved into the decision between curse and blessing.

Amos is the first one to announce a message of Yahweh's judgment over all Israel, a message of which there are examples neither in the clan wisdom of ancient Israel nor in the older central cultic proclamation. So it is not surprising that he does not present his message in the wisdom manner, that is, as a logical consequence within the structure of proverbial wisdom, but rather introduces it regularly as a new, unprecedented word of God, prefaced by the formula "Thus says Yahweh."[195] Amos himself could therefore not accept the statement which was probably added by one of the transmitters culturally related to him:[196]

193. See above, pp. 23 ff.

194. See above, pp. 31 ff.; for a different view on what follows, see W. Zimmerli, *The Law and the Prophets*, trans. R. E. Clements (New York: Harper & Row, 1967). Even the distinction at Exodus 20:5 f. between afflictions striking, at the most, four (contemporaneous) generations of a family and the steadfast love of Yahweh encompassing a thousand generations is probably characteristic for the preprophetic proclamation.

195. See above, note 2.

196. Cf. V. Maag (cited above, note 51), pp. 31, 193 ff.

The prudent one will be silent in that time,
for it is an evil time (5:13).

Our investigation has aimed essentially at explaining the cultural background from which Amos originated and which is determinative for his proclamation. But we will understand his individuality only when we perceive that Yahweh had taken him "from following the flock" (7:15).

What, then, became of the man who was raised on, and skilled in, clan wisdom? Amaziah calls him a "seer" (*ḥōzeh*, 7:12). Even the superscription over his book avoids the word "prophet" and characterizes him as one who "had visions" (*ḥāzāh*, 1:1) over Israel.[197] In his visions (7:1–8; 8:1–2; 9:1–4) his exciting, new commission came to him. It should not immediately be dismissed, but rather further considered, whether Amos is not, by the address as "seer," clearly contrasted with a prophetic office indebted to the cult.[198]

197. In another connection we have already had to allude to the similar linguistic usage in Isa. 30:10 (cf. 1:1; 2:1).
198. Cf. R. Smend (cited above, note 8), p. 417, who regards it worthy of consideration that *ḥōzeh* ("seer") is the proper designation for Amos.

CONCLUSION:

Amos Lives Out of the Oral Tradition of Ancient Israelite Clan Wisdom

In the last analysis, Julius Wellhausen is still entirely correct—at least with reference to Amos[199]—in his assertion that the creed of the prophets does not rest on any book.[200] That holds not only for Amos's pronouncements of judgment (*Gerichtsansage*), but also for his speeches of reproach (*Scheltrede*) used with reference to ancient Israelite law. Ernst Würthwein[201] has polemicized against that point—no doubt incorrectly—even though his own "Amos-Studien" had convincingly demonstrated for the first time the connections between the accusations of Amos and the law handed down in ancient Israel. The course of research, however, was obliged, due to the influence of Robert Bach's conclusions that Amos had actually harked back to only one strand of the ancient Israelite

199. Not so for Hosea; cf. H. W. Wolff, *Hosea* (cited above, note 118), on Hosea 8:11.
200. J. Wellhausen, *Prolegomena zur Geschichte Israels* ([3]1886), p. 417; Eng. trans. by J. S. Black and Allan Menzies, *Prolegomena to the History of Israel* (Edinburgh: A. & C. Black, 1885), p. 399.
201. E. Würthwein (cited above, note 9), pp. 48 ff.

legal tradition, namely, to that of Albrecht Alt's so-called apodictic law,[202] to lead to recognition of the prophet's individuality and continuing influence. Here Erhard Gerstenberger[203] accomplished the decisive step when he showed the lines of connection to the clan ethos.

The original proclamation of ancient Israelite divine law continued in the form of clan wisdom, in an unchangeable manner, at least into the times of Amos, at all events in some circles of Israel still living in a seminomadic state and in their centers of settlement in country towns. That was what our investigation of several particular rhetorical forms, but also of specific contents of the proclamation of Amos, especially sought to show. Above all, however, it should thereby be clarified that Amos was indeed in his basic message a lonely speaker of the prophetic "No" (*Neinsager*), but that also he obviously had a hereditary cultural background of his own. That background, however, is to be sought in none of the great cult centers, but in a particular type of clan wisdom. To identify this more precisely will repay further research.

202. R. Bach (cited above, note 10), pp. 23–24.

203. E. Gerstenberger, *Wesen und Herkunft* (cited above, note 83). In this connection the suggestions made by S. Terrien (cited above, note 26) can be taken up. It is he who for the first time elevated to a theme the subject of this work.

FOR FURTHER READING:

Bibliography of Writings by Hans Walter Wolff and about the Subject of This Book

By Hans Walter Wolff:

Jesaja 53 im Urchristentum. Dissertation, Halle, 1942; first printed, Bethel bei Bielefeld, 1942. Berlin: Evangelische Verlagsanstalt, 3d ed. 1952.

Gesammelte Studien zum Alten Testament. ThB, 22. Munich: Chr. Kaiser, 1964. Includes a dozen essays written 1934–64, among them "Hoseas geistige Heimat" (originally in *TLZ* 81 [1956]: cols. 83–94), pp. 232–50; and "Das Zitat im Prophetenspruch, Eine Studie zur prophetischen Verküngigungsweise" (1937), pp. 36–129.

Dodekapropheton 1 Hosea. BKAT 14/1. Neukirchen-Vluyn: Neukirchener Verlag, 1961; 2d ed. rev. 1965. Eng. trans. forthcoming, Fortress Press, Hermeneia series.

Dodekapropheton 2 Joel/Amos. BKAT 14/2. Neukirchen-Vluyn: Neukirchener Verlag, 1969. Eng. trans. forthcoming, Fortress Press, Hermeneia series.

Hosea 1–7, der Gemeinde ausgelegt. Hosea 8–14, der

Gemeinde ausgelegt. Alttestamentliche Predigten, 4 and 5. Neukirchen-Vluyn: Neukirchener Verlag, 1959 and 1961.

Frieden ohne Ende: Jesaja 7, 1–17 und 9, 1–6 ausgelegt. BSt, 35. Neukirchen-Vluyn: Neukirchener Verlag, 1962.

Die Botschaft des Buches Joel. Theologische Existenz heute, 109. Munich: Chr. Kaiser, 1963.

Wegweisung: Gottes Wirken im Alten Testament. Vorträge zum Bibelverständnis. Munich: Chr. Kaiser, 1965.

Studien zum Jonabuch, mit den Bibelarbeiten des Deutschen Evangelischen Kirchentags Köln 1965. BSt, 47. Neukirchen-Vluyn: Neukirchener Verlag, 1965.

Die Stunde des Amos: Prophetie und Protest. Munich: Chr. Kaiser, 1969.

Bibel—Das Alte Testament. Eine Einführung in seine Schriften und in die Methoden ihrer Erforschung. Bibliothek Themen der Theologie, ed. H. J. Schultz. Stuttgart & Berlin: Kreuz Verlag, 1970. Eng. trans. forthcoming, Fortress Press.

"Das Ende des Heiligtums in Bethel." *Archäologie und Altes Testament: Festschrift für Kurt Galling.* Ed. A. Kuschke and E. Kutsch. Tübingen: Mohr, 1970. Pp. 287–98.

Menschliches—Vier Reden über das Herz, den Ruhetag, die Ehe und den Tod im Alten Testament. Munich: Chr. Kaiser, 1971.

"The Day of Rest in the Old Testament." *Lexington Theological Quarterly* (Lexington, Kentucky) 7 (1972): 65–76.

(Editor). *Probleme biblischer Theologie: Gerhard von Rad zum 70. Geburtstag.* Munich: Chr. Kaiser, 1971. Includes Wolff's "Gespräch mit Gerhard von Rad," pp. 648–58.

Amos and Prophecy (including commentaries on Amos):

BARACKMAN, PAUL F. "Preaching from Amos." *Interpretation* 13 (1959): 296–315.

COHEN, S. "Amos *Was* a Navi." *Hebrew Union College Annual* 32 (1961): 175–78.

CRÜSEMANN, FRANK. "Kritik an Amos im deuteronomischen Geschichtswerk: Erwägungen zu 2. Könige 14:27." In *Probleme biblischer Theologie* (von Rad festschrift, cited above under "Wolff," 1971), pp. 57–63. The "radical No" of Amos was not regarded by the Deuteronomistic historian at 2 Kings 14:27 as word of Yahweh.

GROSCH, HEINZ. *Der Prophet Amos.* Handbücherei für den Religionsunterricht, 6. Gütersloh: Gütersloher Verlagshaus Gerd Mohn, 1969.

HAMMERSHAIMB, ERLING. *The Book of Amos: A Commentary.* Trans. John Sturdy from the 3d ed. of *Amos Fortolket* (1967). New York: Schocken Books, 1970.

HARPER, WILLIAM R. *A Critical and Exegetical Commentary on Amos and Hosea.* International Critical Commentary. New York: Charles Scribner's Sons, 1905.

HOWIE, CARL G. "Expressly For Our Time: The Theology of Amos." *Interpretation* 13 (1959): 273–85.

HYATT, J. P. "The Book of Amos." *Interpretation* 3 (1949): 338–48.

KAPELRUD, ARVID S. *Central Issues in Amos*. Oslo: Oslo University Press, 1961.

KING, PHILIP J. "Amos." *The Jerome Biblical Commentary*. Ed. Raymond E. Brown, S.S.; Joseph A. Fitzmyer, S.J.; Roland E. Murphy, O. Carm. Englewood Cliffs, N.J.: Prentice-Hall, 1968. Section 14, pp. 245–52.

KRAFT, CHARLES F. "The Book of Amos." *The Interpreter's One-Volume Commentary on the Bible*. Ed. Charles M. Laymon. Nashville & New York: Abingdon, 1971. Pp. 465–76.

MCKEATING, HENRY. *The Books of Amos, Hosea and Micah*. Cambridge Bible Commentary on the New English Bible. New York: Cambridge University Press, 1971.

MAYS, JAMES LUTHER. "Words about the Words of Amos: Recent Study of the Book of Amos." *Interpretation* 13 (1959): 259–72.

———. *Amos: A Commentary*. The Old Testament Library. Philadelphia: Westminster, 1969.

MORGENSTERN, JULIUS. *Amos Studies*. Vol. 1. Cincinnati: Hebrew Union College Press, 1941.

RENDTORFF, ROLF. "Reflections on the Early History of Prophecy in Israel." Trans. Paul J. Achtemeier. In Wolfhart Pannenberg et al., *History and Hermeneutic (Journal for Theology and the Church*, 4; ed. R. W. Funk; New York: Harper & Row, 1967), pp. 14–34, especially pp. 19 ff. Originally in *ZTK* 59 (1962): 145–67.

ROWLEY, H. H. "Was Amos a Nabi?" *Festschrift Otto Eissfeldt.* Halle, 1947. Pp. 191–98.

RYAN, D. "Amos." *A New Catholic Commentary on Holy Scripture.* Ed. R. C. Fuller et al. London: Nelson, 1969. Sections 554–60, pp. 693–701.

SMART, JAMES D. "Amos." *The Interpreter's Dictionary of the Bible.* Ed. G. A. Buttrick et al. New York & Nashville: Abingdon, 1962. Pp. 116–21.

SNAITH, NORMAN H. *The Book of Amos. Parts I and II.* Study Notes on Bible Books. London: Epworth, 1945, 1946.

THOROGOOD, BERNARD. *A Guide to the Book of Amos: with Theme Discussions on Judgement, Social Justice, Priest and Prophet.* Theological Education Fund, Study Guides, 4. London: SPCK, 1971.

VOLLMER, JOCHEN. *Geschichtliche Rückblicke und Motive in der Prophetie des Amos, Hosea und Jesaja.* BZAW, 119. Berlin: de Gruyter, 1971.

WARD, JAMES M. *Amos & Isaiah: Prophets of the Word of God.* Nashville & New York: Abingdon, 1969.

WILLI-PLEIN, INA. *Vorformen der Schriftexegese innerhalb des Alten Testaments: Untersuchungen zum literarischen Werden der auf Amos, Hosea und Micha zurückgehenden Bücher im hebräischen Zwolfprophetenbuch.* BZAW, 123. Berlin: de Gruyter, 1971.

WOLFE, R. E. *Meet Amos and Hosea: The Prophets of Israel.* New York: Harper, 1945.

WATTS, JOHN D. W. *Vision and Prophecy in Amos.* Grand Rapids: Eerdmans, 1958.

———. *Studying the Book of Amos.* Nashville: Broadman, 1966.

On the Wisdom Movement:

CRENSHAW, J. L. "The Influence of the Wise on Amos." *ZAW* 79 (1967): 42–51.

GERSTENBERGER, ERHARD. *Wesen und Herkunft des "apodiktischen Rechts."* WMANT, 20. Neukirchen-Vluyn: Neukirchener Verlag, 1965.

LINDBLOM, JOHANNES. "Wisdom in the Old Testament Prophets." In *Wisdom in Israel and in the Ancient Near East. Presented to Professor Harold Henry Rowley. . . . VT* Supplements, 3. Leiden: Brill, 1955. Pp. 192–204.

MURPHY, ROLAND E. "Assumptions and Problems in Old Testament Wisdom Research." *Catholic Biblical Quarterly* 29 (1967): 407–18.

———. "The Interpretation of Old Testament Wisdom Literature." *Interpretation* 23 (1969): 289–301.

———. "Introduction to Wisdom Literature." *Jerome Biblical Commentary* (cited above, under KING, PHILIP J.), section 28, pp. 487–94.

OSTEN-SACKEN, PETER VON DER. *Die Apokalyptik in ihrem Verhältnis zu Prophetie und Weisheit.* Theologische Existenz heute, 157. Munich: Chr. Kaiser, 1969. On Daniel 2, in relation to prophecy and wisdom.

RICHTER, WOLFGANG. *Recht und Ethos: Versuch einer Ortung des weisheitlichen Mahnspruches.* Studien zum Alten und Neuen Testament, 15. Munich: Kösel-Verlag, 1966.

Schmid, H. H. *Wesen und Geschichte der Weisheit: eine Untersuchung zur altorientalischen und Is-raelitischen Weisheitliteratur.* BZAW, 101. Berlin: Alfred Töpelmann Verlag, 1966.

Terrien, Samuel. "Amos and Wisdom." In *Israel's Prophetic Heritage: Essays in Honor of James Muilenberg.* Ed. Bernhard W. Anderson and Walter Harrelson. New York: Harper & Row, 1962. Pp. 108–15.

von Rad, Gerhard. *Old Testament Theology.* Trans. D. M. G. Stalker. New York: Harper & Row. Vol. 1 (1962), pp. 418–59.

———. *Weisheit in Israel.* Neukirchen-Vluyn: Neu-kirchener Verlag, 1970. Traces apocalyptic to wis-dom origins.

Whedbee, J. William. *Isaiah and Wisdom.* New York & Nashville: Abingdon, 1971. Argues that Isaiah employed wisdom traditions in order to oppose the sages in Jerusalem. Discussion of the "woe-cries."

Wood, James. *Wisdom Literature: An Introduction.* Duckworth Studies in Theology, 64. London: Duckworth, 1967.

Zimmerli, Walther. "The Place and Limit of the Wisdom in the Framework of the Old Testament Theology." *Scottish Journal of Theology* 17 (1964): 146–58.

Many important articles and monographs cited in Wolff's footnotes are not repeated in the bibliography above, where the emphasis is especially on titles in English not included in his monograph or on works which have appeared since he wrote in 1964.

LIST OF ABBREVIATIONS

ANET   *Ancient Near Eastern Texts Relating to the Old Testament,* ed. J. B. Pritchard, 3d ed. (Princeton: Princeton University Press, 1969).

ATD   Das Alte Testament Deutsch (Göttingen: Vandenhoeck & Ruprecht).

BH   *Biblia Hebraica,* ed. R. Kittel, 3d ed.

BKAT   Biblischer Kommentar, Altes Testament (Neukirchen-Vluyn: Neukirchener Verlag).

BSt   Biblische Studien (Neukirchen-Vluyn: Neukirchener Verlag).

BWANT   Beiträge zur Wissenschaft vom Alten und Neuen Testament (Stuttgart: Kohlhammer).

BZAW   Beihefte zur Zeitschrift für die alttestamentliche Wissenschaft (Berlin: Töpelmann/de Gruyter).

EvT   *Evangelische Theologie.*

FRLANT   Forschungen zur Religion und Literatur des Alten und Neuen Testaments (Göttingen: Vandenhoeck & Ruprecht).

HAT   Handbuch zum Alten Testament (Tübingen: Mohr).

HBK   Herder's Bibelkommentar (Freiburg: Herder).

JBL   *Journal of Biblical Literature.*

KAT   Kommentar zum Alten Testament (Gütersloh: Gütersloher Verlagshaus Gerd Mohn).

RGG[3]   *Die Religion in Geschichte und Gegenwart,* ed. K. Galling, 3d ed. (Tübingen: Mohr, 1957–65).

RSV   Revised Standard Version of the Bible.

SAT   Die Schriften des Alten Testaments, ed. H. Gunkel et al. (Göttingen).

ThB   Theologische Bücherei (Munich: Chr. Kaiser).

TLZ   *Theologische Literaturzeitung.*

VT   *Vetus Testamentum.*

WMANT   Wissenschaftliche Monographien zum Alten und Neuen Testament (Neukirchen-Vluyn: Neukirchener Verlag).

ZAW   *Zeitschrift für die alttestamentliche Wissenschaft.*

ZTK   *Zeitschrift für Theologie und Kirche.*

Index of Scriptural Passages Cited